EROS AT THE WORLD

KITE PAGEANT

POEMS 1979–1982

MACMILLAN PUBLISHING CO., INC.

New York

COLLIER MACMILLAN PUBLISHERS

London

10/28/05

For Andy
Great pleasure to meet you,
& with ardent thanks for
the lovely tour —
hoping to meet again,
all warmest
regards,
Larry

EROS AT THE WORLD
KITE PAGEANT

POEMS 1979–1982

Laurence Lieberman

Macmillan Publishing Co., Inc.
866 Third Avenue, New York, N.Y. 10022
Collier Macmillan Canada, Inc.

Library of Congress Cataloging in Publication Data

Lieberman, Laurence.
    Eros at the world kite pageant.

    I. Title.
PS3562.I43E7   1983   811'.54   82–14898
ISBN 0–02–571860–6
ISBN 0–02–069810–0 (pbk.)

10   9   8   7   6   5   4   3   2   1

Eros at the World Kite Pageant is also published in a hardcover edition by Macmillan Publishing Co., Inc.

Printed in the United States of America

for my wife, Binnie,
and in memory of
James Wright

Contents

Acknowledgments

I wish to thank the Illinois Arts Council and the Center for Advanced Study at the University of Illinois for Creative Writing Fellowships, which provided me with indispensable time for completing the poems in this book.

I thank the editors of the following magazines, in which these poems first appeared:

American Poetry Review:	"Psychodrama: Tokyo Mime Film"
	"Lament for the Doomed Minnows"
	"The Protectors: Oak and Stone"
	"The Roof Tableau of Kashikojima"
	"The Tilemaker's Hill Fresco"
	"Eros at the World Kite Pageant"
	"Moonlighters"
The Chariton Review:	"On the Life That Waits"
	"Song of the River Sweep"
The Chicago Review:	"Worming into the Boulder Caves"
The Hudson Review:	"The Grave Rubbings"
The Kansas Quarterly:	"Soba Noodles and Gun Buffs"
Michigan Quarterly Review:	"Two Koto Songs"
The Nation:	"Saltcod Red"
The New England Review:	"Loves of the Peacocks"
	"Yokosuka Churl"
The New Yorker:	"Ago Bay: The Regatta in the Skies"
Quarterly West:	"Two Songs of Leave-Taking"
	"Ode to the Runaway Caves"
The Sewanee Review:	"Purgatory: The Antiaircraft Screen"
Tar River Poetry:	"Dominican Shoe Tinkers"
Wisconsin Review:	"Enoshima Tide Pools"

ON THE LIFE THAT WAITS

(for James Wright)

I.

How odd it is. For a week I have lived
among trees, many long thin straight ones. They shine.
If they could they would love each other.
It may be they do.
They stick up their tops, just outside my window.
And I do not know the touch of bark
to my fingers.
The smell of leaves in my nose.
In my ears, no crackle of branches.
Nor a pull of roots at my feet. Roots.
I have sat here, and looked.
And wondered.
I think well of myself and what I write,
sometimes. But I do not know these trees.
Can I say I live?

II.

When I look again, the people come.
How I long to touch them.
Not only in special places, but those too.
I would make them quiver with life.
Their own life. And mine,
of course. The music would be in everyone's ears
like sap in the trees.
And grass.
They have not just come. They have always been here.
And they mean to stay.
These people.
If I cannot see my face in their eyes
it is a sadness.

III.

It is important to look close
if you think it is. Yes.
And just now we do.
There are toothmarks all over this branch.
I do not ask, is it woodpeckers or squirrels? The teeth are sharp.

[1]

They do as they are bidden.
I have the proof.
When I come to chew my branch
may I have such teeth.

1. SONGS OF LEAVE-TAKING

PSYCHODRAMA: TOKYO MIME FILM

Korean
Lady mime,
    you suspend yourself beside the stunned
    Caucasian seated
        at table, waiting to order his meal,

his fate.
You will teach
    him, wordlessly, about the void. Propped
    on an invisible chair,
        one leg crossed over the other, sipping

coffee,
your finger
    curled in genteel crook around the handle
    of a nonexistent
        cup, you drop two missing lumps of sugar,

stirring
with a spoon
    of air. He, pretending to ignore you—
    secretly befuddled—
        thinks he fears your sex, not guessing

the threat
is your one
    possession: absence, the widening hole
    in space torn by your id
        turning itself inside out, eating

its way,
shadowily,
    into everything solid around it. . . .
    Now you dance. You pirouette,
        spinning, weaving with your hands. You wrap him in

vacancy
and he cannot
    refuse it—it is his own silence you draw
    from him, strand by silken
        strand: a cocoon in which you wind and bind him.

TWO KOTO SONGS

I.

On the Yokohama
Express, the box fills a row of three seats
and protrudes
  into the aisle, perhaps two feet of overhang
   to be dodged by commuters
  filing through the gates. Traffic—
    luckily!—is light. . . .

  At the taxi-stand,
three cabbies protest, shooing us out the rear—
we rotating
  the case inside compact Toyotas to secure
   the best angle for transport.
  Diagonally. Front
   to rear. Top to bottom,

   across shoulders, laps.
Left to right, overshooting half an arm's length
through both windows.
  Or extending upwards from the floor, pointing
   through one window, at a wide
  high angle, half again
   higher than the whole car,

   towering over hardtop
roof. The fourth driver accepts a double-fare
bribe: speeding—
  sadistically—he ignores the backseat struggles,
   our shuffling the box to avoid
  hitting utility
   poles, a low-hanging

   traffic signal, two
ducking jay-walkers. Nearly sideswiping a truck,
all but clouting
  an atypically tall officer in the neck
   directing traffic, Doug Stout

in back twists the box—
   an elephant gun

  or hockey stick?—to miss
unwanted targets, Toshi in front waving
his crutches
   to signal mid-lane cruisers on the turns
    and occasional passing
  speeders (slow traffic safe
    in the inside lanes). . . .

II.

You bend
to the task
   as masseuse kneels to her healing labors.
   With a motion of kneading
    and caressing at once, you stroke waves of sound

into thin-
layered skin
   of the laminated boards, though you touch
   only the few exposed nerve-vines.
    You draw your curled wands across the taut strings,

a cradling
motion, hands
   pulling inward to your breast. Your fingers,
   capped with ivory picks (*tsume*,
    jacketing the digits with mother-of-pearl: false

fingernails),
pluck from each
   yards-long fiber of spun cat innards low wails. . . .
   From the coffin of air, moans
    and lamentings. The single clear cries are stolen—

beautiful
thieveries!—filched
   from each string as fire is purloined from flint.
   Sparks flying like shooting stars
    from axe-head honed at the grinding wheel. Splinters

and smoke,
fine wedges of bark,
    springing from blows of the axe chopping logs.
    Sticks of incense consumed,
      burnt up in their own self-fueled conflagrations,

hatching
dumb solid chalks
    into aromatic mists and scents. A voice
    of fire may be struck from each
      still form; from each dull inanimate shape, chantings! .

The hidden
songs may be plucked
    by skilled hand from the Japanese long harp
    laid flat to the floor—a pillow
      of oak, finding its voice in a hardwood sleep.

ENOSHIMA TIDE POOLS

1. Nikon Studies

Two young native
women, marathon sunbathers, loll
in the same poolside nook
    for hours. Soporific, flat-chested,
    they lie supine on thin limbs
without contour—magnetic
    despite absence of figure. Sprawled
at right angles to each other,
they are withdrawn, immobile and shapeless
    as torpid slugs. Full-grown, they seem no taller
      than two pre-teen
      American sisters, knobby

      and loose-jointed,
    engrossed in horseplay with their towhead
kid brother in the pool
    adjacent to the somnolent pair. . . .
    The lanky, older child
approaches the sun-
    tranced duo. Leaning on one knee,
half-stooped, she addresses
a few words to the nearer mate, who sits up,
    rising halfway to meet her—spare torso braced
      on one forearm
      extended to her side. . . . I,

      slowly circling
    behind them, unnoticed, Nikon upraised,
catch all three in a charmed
    pose, starkly silhouetted—in profile—
    against a gleaming backdrop,
a tall rock pillar.
    The two seated figures exchange
covert eyeflicks—drollery
in their half-closed lashes: the one invoked,
    gathering a number of wrinkled transparent sacks
      from the rock seat,
      passes them to the upright

spindly child,
who springs back to her expectant siblings.
Aided by the plastic scoops,
        gifts from their aloof sun-absorbed neighbors,
        our three anglers dunk and pounce
in tide pools. They bag
        a swift quarry of minnows, inchling
mackerel and yellowtail,
spidery crayfish and tiny squids. . . . I step
        backwards, my camera's zoom lens now aimed
            at the stooped
            performers—it is a tableau

            from a silent
film, circa nineteen-nineteen, the figures
grown unfamiliar, estranged
        in an alien landscape, their high-pitched
        voices muted and blent
with the whine of sea
        wind, the rumble of swells. Three hyper-
active younglings, ceaseless,
a tribe of deft elves, their limbs a whirring
        blur—all energy and motion—they could whip up
            spindrift into curds.
            Or subdivide the molecules

            of shore tars,
        decomposing crab claws, gull skulls—and sew
them into nets, woven
        skeletal tapestries, tied with ribbons
        of kelp, or green-black bands
of nori seaweed
        shredded from local crops nearing mid-
summer harvest in offshore
waters of neighboring Miura Peninsula,
        adjacent to Enoshima's east shore. Conjurors,
            these American
            junior expatriates re-mix

            the elements
        to suit their wits' wizardry, rearrange
compounds of sand and skin,

leaf and shell, flint and surf . . . I step back,
again, and refocus the lens.
Their flapping arms
are wings, their mobile legs—flexing,
unflexing—ruffled tail feathers
of shore terns and scoters, low skimmers
flying so close to surfaces . . . sand . . . water . . . rock,
all feather ends
seem to nip or scrape floors—

but none do touch.
So fleet and arrowy, these prancing feather-
weights are true human kin
to thin-boned delicate shore birds. But here,
in this littoral humankind
beach panorama,
they are a trio of misfits, freaks,
metabolic anomalies. . . .
I survey the nearby glittering rock flats,
small crater-shaped pools scattered to outlying
coastlines, all shore
limits. Everywhere I glance,

my eye settles
on creatures of leisure. I view a populace
of loiterers, dreamy
hangers-on: some linger, arm-locked, in pairs;
others straddle ledges,
in family clusters;
a few solitaries, idling down strand
or coast-ridge, seem to peer
at their own faces in standing pools,
Narcissuslike. The very breath, or blood tempo,
of all common
earthlings is slow pace, slower. . . .

2. Two Blood Tempos

Now supine, now
prone, the sister recluses—a prostrate Race—
sink into declivities,
sloped hollows of rock in which their slim hips
and shoulders are cradled.

Their thin frames match
    bone shafts and delicate flesh mounds
to exact-fit cushions
and gulleys of the stony mattress, torsos
    curled in their partial cocoon sacs as worm larvae
      are wrapped in slick-
      ooze envelopes. Their necks and spines

      wriggle closer
    and closer to a perfect blend with shore
contours—their slow bloods seek
    immersion in the bondless slick surfaces.
    Inured to unceasing wave-wash.
Or bake of sun-blaze.
    Inwound and bud-curled, they would absorb
all the world's slaps and sucks.
Two cultured pearls, hid in tight shells, inlaid. . . .
    Our three children, mercurial, fish-scale shimmer
      in their eyes—hot bloods
      erupt, at one with whipped streams,

      flailings across
    rock. *A spirit of silveriness. Star points*
of sun flashed in flung drops.
    Lit flares one second, doused sparks the next.
    Three hyper-imps, wading deep,
they are scouting for fish
    near the wide pool's center. They divide
the pool face into pie slice
wedges, a right-to-left circuit of near-equal
    shares. Now each rush of their counterclockwise
      surveillance turns up
      more victims of the shrunk infant

      fish population—
    mounting cheers of the hunt drawing the aloof,
stoic beauties from seclusion.
    Soon, both charmschool belles, now agitated,
    hover over three bobbing heads
of the children—their poised
    thin stick figures upright, swaying.
They applaud each fresh capture
with hand claps and half-muffled whickerings

followed by high-pitched short whinnies, squeaks. . . .
   Later, they are stooped,
   tittering, in awkward sexual

      poses (wholly lapsed
  out of their stupor of loftiness), their limbs
undergoing a polka
   of painful stretches and bends, while they shift
   from close-kneed crouch to spread-
legged squat. Nearly splits!
   Wincing, they take gingerly steps
along the jagged rim—
prickly to toe pads, foot soles—of a lopsided
   quadrilateral, the smallish tide pool adjacent
     to the egg-shaped
     pond worked by the teenagers, who,

      taking a rest break
  from their sport, observe with much fascination
their belated allies
   in the hunt (as do I, unnoticed yet, Nikon
   aimed at my comely models). . . .
Suddenly, I perceive
   the two opposite blood poles reverse,
shift to a common level,
the Japanese nymphs moving, by short fluttery
   hops—furtive as jays—inching around and around
     the squarish water hole,
     cupping their hands for scootaway

      fish, near misses
  at best, but glowing with pleasure in the chase. . . .
Carla offers to return, gratis,
   the unused pair of fish traps (her siblings, lulled,
   meandering toward shore to seek
odd finds—pitted crab husks,
   whorled shells); but the lithe couple,
with polite demurs, refuse
the gift. We leave them in mid-pool, buried in water
   to their chins, waving to us, but dunking their heads
     for underwater
     skirmishes—between *sayonaras.*

3. Lament for the Doomed Minnows

Debra groans!—
her fish pets, she fears, are dying from lack
of oxygen. . . . Our huntress
and huntsman—two wiry vagabonds—stall
to inspect the translucent-bodied
minnows through plastic sides
of their fish traps, small bloated
water balls. Idly, I stroll
to nearest inland loop of shoreline,
bend to flowing tongue of sea, then dunk
our just-emptied,
large picnic zipper-satchel

filling it
quickly with quarts of pure sea spillage,
and declare: "Take this. A fish
preserve. Unlimited oxygen for dozens
of displaced baby sea waifs. . . ."
Our long hike ended, we
embark on a last short trek,
the quarter-mile-long
promenade across Bentembashi
Causeway (a concrete bridge joining
Enoshima Isle
to the mainland), dallying some

to allow Debra
time-out to transfer the most tiny few
gasping minnows from undersized
baglets to improvised new fish tub,
my makeshift aquarium.
Delicately, she gropes
for pulsing infant fry, ashimmer,
no larger than tadpoles,
her fingertips gently pinching
together—like surgical tweezers—
while she marvels
at the frail beauty of mini-finned

larvalike flakes:
creatures whose scales, thin as mica leafs,

brush off at a lightest touch—
  sparkling like sequins on fingernails,
  or outlined sharply *within* grooves
of fingerprint whorls.
  The smallest of this brood, pasted
to inner surfaces
of thin plastic, cling to the seams,
    resist her fingers' most intricate strokes
      and pryings—
      the fishbabies' near-invisible

      hides seem molded
  to the very substance of vinyl,
inseparably. She is moved
    to tears, fearful lest she crush the last
    fishlets in her rage to save them
from suffocation
    (*she has read about gills, piscine*
modes of breathing
in the scaly aquatic phylum—
      if she could, she'd transplant bits, cells,
        sacs of her lungs
        into their breasts, and teach them how

      to breathe air) . . . .
    "Now they're homesick for follow kinfish,"
she grieves—running to the bridge
    railing, she shakes out the bags held open-
    mouthed over swift-flowing currents
below. But the lone strays
    won't come loose for all her tries
to dislodge them, for all
her chanted sweet lullabies—
    "Babyfish, babyfish, dive away home,"
      liltingly sung
      in familiar *ladybird* refrain. . . .

      She turns the bags
    inside out, finally, the minnows glued
stuck to seams, and she—chary
    to tweak or pinch them for fear of injury
    to gills or delicate insides—

drops both sacks, flopping
    end over end in the wind to sea
wash under the bridge, sighing
her relief as they fall homeward. But no!
    One bag, flying back into the bridge pile,
        fastens to stone—
           waif frozen to a fossil grave.

WORMING INTO THE BOULDER CAVES

(for Robert Penn Warren)

Nearing the island's foot—
in slow descent from the summit—we follow
a rich dirt path invaded by strips and rhomboids of bare rock
usurping more and more of the narrow trail,
raised mounds a hazard we must dodge
to keep from tripping,
            finally, on the steep last drop-off
to sea level, the children
            bounding down the rocky chute to the bottom: a floor

            of glassy marbled-grey rock—
is it black ice containing bubbles, pockets
and swirls of foam?—leaps up to meet our braking sandals! We skid,
our hands frantically knuckling a last pillar
of stone where the walkway dissolves
into a vast shelf
            of sparkly wet slate. All flora—
grown wispier and sparser
            during the last sheer slope of declivity—has vanished:

            leaf, stem, or blossom shrunk
to sapless crinkles; vine-lace of wisteria
shrivelled to brittle threads. We survey the sandless, beachless
expanse—from West to East, a waste shore plain
of volcanic glass. It stretches
a hundred meters
            across the black plateau to the breakwater
shore-wall which intercepts
            humped swells before they can mature into wave-caps

            and frothy surf. But the air
is awash with invisible spindrift. . . . Clucks
and snickers warbled overhead! No lone gull or hawk in view,
the familiar chortles—muted and unsuppressed,
by turns—circulate at a height,
whizzing over our ears. . . .
            A great knobby boulder—streaked with algae
and brine, barnacled in patches
            scattered above and below, perhaps thirty feet wide—

looms top-heavy with a crown
slanting over our shoulders. I spy three pairs
of unlaced sneakers cast aside beneath the stone eminence.
Two bobbing sets of ears pop in and out
of view, followed by hunched backs:
children scuttling
              on all fours—surefooted as mountain goats,
they hop over slick ledges
              flanking the crest. Our louts! My protests blurted

       too late at the blank rock
colossus. . . . All three—wormlike—go tunnelling
into high sockets, threading slim hips and limbs into the caves.
Now we hear voices circuiting swiftly within—
right to left, diagonally. Up
and down. Front to rear.
       The divers search ghostly chambers
of a vast honeycomb
              of linked caves radiating in all directions—

       all interconnected—
through the giant stone's upper reaches
and outermost limits, their hoots and squawks ranging from a level
just over our heads to a cliff-top balcony
four times our height. Imps or trolls—
one after another—
       they flash their faces at us, teasing, eyes
adazzle with wicked
     gaiety and risk: each glares for a split second

       from a dormer, or arched
cupola, near the rock's peak—then vanishes!
Their voices, high aloft, race each other through the channels.
For a moment, they become stationary,
all three whickering in chorus
from a midway vantage
       at dead center of the cave labyrinth.
We below—amazed listeners—
       fancy a central space, a broad spherical hollow

       or conduit, where all
inner cavities and passageways converge.
The children play out a variety of calls, whistles, tootings—

the medley of sounds and echoes resonates
in all caves of the honeycomb,
though the gay voices
　　　　are stalled in one place. . . . Now three spelunkers
emerge—one by one—hatched
　　　　from hidden exits. They recover the paired sneakers.

SOBA NOODLES AND GUN BUFFS

Tempura bar to one side, soba kitchen
to the other, we bypass
shrimp and noodle treats—lured by staccato
poppings and howls of pleasure issuing
from the narrow store-front
in the middle. Preceded
by a gallop of children, my cheek is
gently stung by two
soft, airborne tan-colored missiles
freezing me in the tall doorway,
my arm upraised to shield my eyes. I peep
between spread fingers, caught
in a crossfire of flying corks showering
down on our heads from all sides, several
bouncing across the doorsill
and rolling over the walkway
outside. Some two or three dozen children,
ranging from toddlers
to late-teen gun buffs, are lined
up helter-skelter in rows
two to three deep, all firing compressed-air
repeater popguns at once,
tall gunners discharging munitions
over the heads of hips-high marksmen in front:
the short patrons (second-
generation novitiates)
unloading short-barreled hand guns and snub-
nosed revolvers; those
in the rear sporting long-range
telescopic rifles, double-
barreled, aimed at targets a few meters
distant. . . . Infants in the fore—
some leaning far over the counter, others
lying full-length on their bellies—place gunbarrels
point blank against prizes
of their choice, taking cross-eyed
care not to dislodge, or overturn, targets
before pulling triggers.

All wins are disqualified
        if not toppled by direct hits
            from popped corks, the only game rule (among ten
    posted regulations)
strictly enforced by a quartet of hostesses
        scurrying to and fro, on both sides
            of the counter. They divide
                their time between distributing
                    prizes to shootists who have deposed targets
                        from their shallow cardboard
                    thrones (ceramic squatting frogs,
                tall princes and longhaired princesses
            carved from coarse-grained knotty plywood, cotton
    flop-eared bunnies), and chasing
the hopelessly scattered hail of runaway corks
        spraying contestants and spectators alike—
            a fireworks display: many corks
                rebounding back into faces
                    of those who released them; others ricocheting
                        over the high partitions
                    between stores of the tri-fronted
                joint concession, splashing in a bowl
            of soba noodles broth, say, or pickle
        relish salad; the cork-ball
condiments falling from kitchen skies
        not quite passing for stale— if spongy—croutons.
            The chief proprietress
                collecting all recoverable
                    rifle ammo in a single wide-brimmed wicker
                        basket, replenishes
                    the munitions stockpile. . . .
                Our triad of sharpshooters,
            of middling height, waver between front lines
        and rear guard: Carla mastering,
first, the counter belly-flop steal, wins
    an outsize share of our family glut of spoils,
        amassing some twenty-
            odd small molded statuettes
                and carved figurines; her two younger teammates
                    securing but three gifts each,
                rudimentary squeakless
            mice (commonest token prizes,

won by every entrant—the poorest shots
in the house). . . . At moments,
I'd felt odd revulsion from the cheats
who poked gunbarrels into the gaudy loins
of statuettes lusted
after—our two small gunners,
paled by my squeamish ethics, played fair
and lost out. Big sister,
swept up into the maelstrom
of local hustler-shootists, scores
a bonanza, tying the super-Blitz house record
for statuary filched
in one hour. The ranking, matronly hostess,
hot in our pursuit, bears in the crook of each arm
two Grand Prizes bedecked
with ornamental curlicues
and filigree. She offers to exchange both
special presentos—
the tall upright angel
and the silver-plated historic
cannon—for twenty small dolls and figurines.
It's bargain. Lucky trade.
Good swap. She explains in pidgin English,
patchily—a ritual spiel—how local townfolks'
skilled junior gunners
save up their nominal midget
prizes, interim trinkets, to barter at week's
end for art treasures—
each month's favorite monument
of historic or priestly value,
crafted by Zen Buddhists or secular workers
in clay, hardwood, soft metals
or woven fabric. The children, held tranced
by this exotic prattle, bow and mutter
politest no-thank-yous. . . .
We five each carrying off
armfuls of loot, I let slip a frail gilded
swan, its wing-tips
chipping. Carla drops a puffed-up
black-and-white panda, but she catches
it, intact, on her soft moccasin-type loafer,
retrieves the fallen Teddy

and fixes it more securely atop the load—
a pyramid she now balances, asway. . . .
She glides—as if afloat
on roller skates—out the exit.

PURGATORY:
THE ANTIAIRCRAFT SCREEN

Are they Jap Zeroes or Yank
      Spitfires? . . . The antiaircraft
missiles are fired
        at nondescript planes
        in the rifle range. You, *Gaijin*,
and the *Nijonjin* locals get equal

bloodthirsty thrills from gunning
      them down as, one by one,
they stagger
        like wounded doves,
        wavery. Or, stalled like blimps—
zeppelins hitting a wind pocket—

they give the kids a moment's leeway
      to adjust their gunsights
on the spectral
        grey-white fuselages
        crawling across blinking slate-grey
skies of the target screen. Each child,

pressing the trigger-button inset
      at the end of a half-moon
steering wheel,
        shouts "A hit!"
        while a pale-yellow light flashes
from the midsection of the victim

aircraft (a wounded firefly squid's
      last flicker of bio-
luminescence
        one moment before—or
        after?—death by speargun), then fades. . . .
The glass-faced quadruped is God

YOKOSUKA CHURL

Slept three days. Two nights. But the blind, deaf & dumb stubborn ox
of your body plodded right on through the massive overdose

of assorted tablets. Two days and three nights of staying awake
now finds you downing tall flask after flask of hot *sake,*

failed antidote for the half-emptied box of telltale prophylactics
you snared in the closet. She left three times before—for weeks,

days?—the broken promise muffled in alibis had sealed your lips.
Oh, Carl, buffalo *mensch,* Saint Churl, you manage an apartment complex

in Yokohama, twelve years good standing. Former plainclothes detective.
San Francisco's North Beach. Six foot four. Two hundred seventy five.

Mountainous *sake*-barrel-paunch. How have you come by your immoderate
gentleness to low-caste geishas—what a passion for touching all delicate

creatures softly! A match for leonine Roethke and his glasshouse minimals!
Poetry? Your ardent love for Housman and Kipling erupts in burbles,

but your eyes inflame when I helplessly croak to hear you adore
McKuen, and your banal apologies for how drunk you are wax obscure.

The Yokosuka bar girls—wowed by your immaculate, fluent Japanese
and your strange reverence for *all* females—are dizzied by your size

oddly coupled with restraint. A genius to not ever hurt woman-flesh.
That vat of blubbery destructive power you hold, always, in check!

I hear you buckle behind me, crashing through the shoji doors. I'm paralyzed.
Frozen, I can't pivot to help you. Now you're knocking your hips and knees

into a tall tin pail, falling and hefting yourself up at once. . . . Parting vows.
In an hour, you'll pull yourself together. Take a train home. I mustn't

worry about you. You wave good-bye ("sure wish you'd try a little harder
to like McKuen"). . . . *Going to find the world's softest lips in Honky Tonk bar!*

[25]

LOVES OF THE PEACOCKS

(Enoshima Zoo)

The sawdust-spattered plank floor is a stage:
                                        three small peahens drop
to their bellies at the erect bird's feet
                        and cower, their wings incurled—a seamless blend
                                        with their shrinking posteriors.
                        The male peafowl
        opens and closes his iridescent wings,
                                        slowly, rising on his toes;
his chest swells, his wings a pump
                        or bellows inflating his trunk and lengthy abdomen,
                                        by gradual puffs. We hear
                        a faint hissing . . .
He squints his eyes, and swiftly unfolds
                                        the many loose webs
of his gorgeously elongated tail plumes
                        into a broad half-moon-shaped aquamarine fan!—
                                        tripling the peafowl's height,
                        a ten or twelve
foot feather-span nearly filling the cage.
                                        His eyeslits appear
to close as scores of gold ocelli flash
                        and shimmer, perhaps four or five eyespots spaced
                                        out over each long tail feather.
                        Now the whole
        tail shudders, the many eyes doubling,
                                        splitting into multiples
of gold flecks—thousands of unblinking irises
                        stipple the ribbons of greeny iridescence fluttering
                                        from the base of each quill
                        to the fork-tipped
        feather ends. . . .
                                The three still hens, their plumage
                                        tucked under folded wings,
lie prostrate, softly clucking, entranced
                        by the prince's spell.
                                        He is agitated, and his high
                                feather-tops start vibrating,

[26   ]

fiercely, like a row
of struck tuning forks while he turns and turns,
            displaying front and rear:
in backview, he partly closes his tail,
    as if to tease; tail widespread in frontview
              (is he keeping time to music?) —
      he pivots and struts,
  again and again. . . .
         Eros or Narcissus, who is
          his muse? I ask. *A courtship*
ritual, you reply.
      A last pirouette!
Now dancing in place, he bobs up and down on tiptoe,
        arching his broad cobra-hood
    of tail forward
over the grovelling peahens' heads; their long necks,
          slithering from side
to side, scrape the gritty floor—scratch-sounds
      blended with a chorus of low dull moans. Now the hens
        contract their tails and wings
      yet again,
  as if trying to suck all of their appendages
           back into the foetal torso-
hoop that budded them forth before birth,
    and roll every stray feather into a perfect ball. . . .
      A volley of tremors, radiating
      from the floor
planks, racks their prone bodies in waves:
          each long shudder starts
with twitches and shakes of their undersides,
    and the charge—overspreading their backs and necks—
        flows upwards into arched pinions
    of Apollo Cock
suspended above them (spreadwinged, he hovers
        a few inches over the floor),
whose tail feathers, now brushing the cage-roof,
    are given at last to such vigorous fluttering
        they become an incandescent blur.
    A *halo arc.*
Rainbow-hued. Rainbow-curved. . . .
              The shimmering border
      highlights the many-webbed fan
of tail, which shades the croaking hens

nestled below, but illuminates the upper third
and outermost corners of stall:
flashing opal-

essence. . . .
The colors keep changing, gold flares
winking on a blue-green backdrop,
white flares on orange, chartreuse on white:
now one color flames out, now another.
A brightest last flareup!
All lights
die at once. The many colors fade . . .
The cage—
it had doubled in size—is shrunk,
but the peahens, springing to their feet, win back
their full-feathered buxom physiques; while the grand
tail fan of the prince
had collapsed,
folded upon itself, shrivelling to less, less
than a shut accordion's flatness:
a moment's pinprick has punctured the swashbuckler's
glory-plumes, and he squats . . .
The hens,
cackling merrily, drive him
into a corner,
strutting and pecking his thin crown.
Next cage.
A second plumed Casanova
commences his display over a reclining cellmate.
Ah! Both heads wear crests
of upright tufts. *Plumelets.*
Which twin
is the wooer? I ask. *Which twin wooed? . . .*

THE PROTECTORS: OAK AND STONE

Strolling up to Nandaimon
(Great South Gate), we flinch, sidestepping
to make way for a scowling thirty-foot-tall
muscle-bound giant, glaring at an enemy
behind us (not ourselves, please God!)....

The lifelike oaken Colossus—carved by Unkei
or his son Tankei,
who otherwise carved the twin Kongo-Rikishi
guardian in the opposite wall (whichever,
each assisted by no
fewer than sixteen
apprentice sculptors)—stomps and tramples a puny devil

underfoot writhing decadent
agonies. Both guardsman and underdog
demon, filling a hollowed-out niche,
stand *inside* the wall, the Goliath poised for a pounce.
"He's on our side, *our* caretaker,"

I say, but hunching my shoulders, I dart past
with nervous quicker step,
accosted a moment later by savage curs,
crouching stone watchdogs recessed in a rear niche
of the same wall: half-
leonine, half-wolfish;
the roughhewn imported stone blocks that hatched them lugged

by four *Sung* men from China
who carved— I swear it!—visible snarls,
growlings the unbespectacled eyes can *hear.* "These,
too, if you please, are in league to have us," I wail,
slackening to a slow run....

TWO SONGS OF LEAVE-TAKING

I. Kamakura

The Mitsubishi fridge
and Nippon-Sears small automatic washer
are earmarked
    to T.; "space" heaters—gas, oil & electric—
      tagged for N.; ironing board,
    vacuum & bedding
        for C., plus two bags

      of snarly clothes and toys
for the poor. . . . We hire a truck, then map out
deliveries
    to friends and needy alike. In just one hour,
      we go to meet our ship.
    Monks of a local
        Zen-Buddhist sect

      come to our door to pay
their last respects. They sing rich chants for us—
that nasal
    humming and groaning (how can there be so much
      vibration in those low,
    shuddery intonings?)—
        all bow! But then,

      without interrupting
the music, a front fold of each grey rough-wool
plain kimono
    is gracefully lowered toward me. I
      drop my coins therein.
    Each fold is lifted—
        raised back up, slowly,

      in the same unbroken
rhythm, the coins jingling in deep pleats, below.
My little son,
    too, makes his offering, dazzled by the monks'
      performance. Clink, clink. *His lead*
ten-yen bus tokens, sound-
        less, are falling still. . . .

II. Yokohama Dock

Toshi is waving his crutch
high—oh, high!—over all heads, needling through
the spaghetti
    webwork of streamers. Now Mrs. Tamura
        has leapt upon Mr.
Tamura's back, and both
        are waving to us—

        to the lost United
States buried in us—waving with that circular
spinning motion,
    the hand call to meet again, meet again,
        oh, anyplace on earth!
Our ship is upborne
        less by sea than by

        our friends' orchestrations.
They are the conductors of a stately music,
their hands batons
    moving to a cadence of benignity—
        we but the choristers
who follow their commands.
        They bid our choir

        the good voyage. . . . But song
in my ears at the last is dear Mr. Niikura's
telephone
    blessings our final two days: "Phone me, or I
        you, for anything, nothing,
today, tomorrow, today,
        again and again. . . ."

II. KASHIKOJIMA QUARTET

AGO BAY: THE REGATTA IN THE SKIES

I.

For hours, our Pullman (half sleeper,
    half parlor car), crammed with vagabond backpackers
       and holiday executives,
burrows into denser clotted passages of Ise-Shima National Park,
    the woods often crowding the tracks
so narrowly we seem to be boring a tunnel as we advance, pine boughs
       and foliage coalescing
behind us. . . . Flashes of blue glitter, to our left
and below; the woods thin out; stretches of aquamarine run together
    in a continuous unwound ribbon flanking
our descent to sea level—the parallel band grows wider,
       suddenly leaping alongside
the tracks and flowing, at last, in a bright tributary below us
    deepening to turquoise, bottom rocks

glinting in the shallows. We climb a short overpass, our tracks
    an elevated scaffoldwork
    flung across trestles, and we burst into the clearing,
forest walls falling away on both sides in a swiftly widening V

    at our backs. Ahead, we bisect
a long isthmus—propped on our raised causeway—yoking
    the wooded landmass
to a narrowing funnel of pasturage. *Goats and calves graze.*
    A stray bull lopes up to the train,
springs back with a grimace, horns upraised for attack. . . . Water
    to left and right,
    all woods left far behind—a shrunken blur—
we seem to gain speed as we traverse the contracting strip
    of land, hastening toward land's
end, our destination, Kashikojima, the town
    fixed to the tip
of the peninsula, a great jetty curved like a boot toe to fit
    the looping contour of shore.

The train seems aimed to overshoot town, docks, the coastline
    mishmash of urban
    and nautical traffic—our engine may vault
the lovely outlying islands! . . . Spray from Ago Bay, saturated

with scents of pearl-oyster beds
and Nori-seaweed, floods in upon our nostrils—and now
flowery jasmines, lilacs,
sea-grapes, as the wind shifts. Mountain breezes give way to sea gusts
billowing up from the bay. We advance
to the forward car, maneuvering to view the approach to Pearl World.
An island-studded seaway
rushes to meet us, the miniaturist color-engraving
on a postage stamp of moments before, pulling us into its ballooning
enclave. The maritime scene expands
into a panoramic bustle of countless land and sea vessels. . . .
Exiting from the train,
I check my footing—the platform sinks a few inches, pitching
this way and that. Seaweed tufts—

sweeping across the city-long quay, blown in eddies,
commingled with lines
and cables of ship moorings—now settle
on the multiple decks of tri-leveled luxury steamboats. . . .

II.

Passing under one low arch
of railroad viaduct—
at right angles to the pier and dock-yard—we seek out
the buried hamlet.
We thirst for contact with townspeople,
the local populace! . . . Scouting for an urban interior,

we track uncertain footpaths
up a steep hillside.
The summit, a broad mesa, stretches to the horizon—
silhouetted on the sky,
a few marshmallow cloud puffs, rushing
to keep pace with jibs and spinnakers, match the sails

for size; flanking the low trim hulls,
the cloud balls unravel
tails and tatters flaring out behind them,
their sister-sails intact,
but forward edges luffing from time to time
in the strong headwinds. Cloud and canvas ride

the same fierce currents. . . . We stroll
across the raised
plateau, arm-linked, enchanted by the regatta
in the skies. The bay surface,
dismantled by the sun's glare, grows
invisible. We advance for a detailed view—the sea,

a mirror now, doubles the fleet
of clouds into two tiers,
an echelon above, twin echelon below.
We behold the spectacle
of white spheroids, ruffled quadrilaterals,
and cupped triangles converging—amassed and fluctuant—

upon the horizon. Ascending into a bloom
of thunderheads, banked
and swelling in the east, the whole galaxy
of vessels and frayed cloudlets—
airborne—swept past the quartermoon's
pale crescent, flies higher and higher. . . .

THE ROOF TABLEAU OF KASHIKOJIMA

An hour's uphill trudge leaves us milling about
  on the flat-topped peak of Cape
Goza, more weary of matchless sea gorge,
  overhang and declivity than shrine
    or Buddha. Absently, I
      glance across the peninsula—
        I'm brought up short: Kashikojima-shi,
         the hidden village,
      is stratified at all levels
    of a forested broad foothill,
    oddly globular—topless pumpkin!—far side
  rimming the opposite coast.
Shifting features of a lit Jack-o'-lantern's
  carved face, hinted by gleams of ceramic tile
    roofs, wink successively—
      sun's glare shuttling through gaps
        in passing clouds. The dwellings are scattered
        at various sites
      of hillslope: near ground level,
    the lowest stratum comprises
  a few geometrically shaped, grey offices
interspersed with modest huts.
Those bungalows facing the sea are graced
  with gallery or portico; the foursquare
    lodgings facing inland,
      diminutive, bare, are stripped of all
        outward appurtenances. Halfway up the bluff,
        we discern in wooded
      groves a pair of *Minshiku*—
    half inn, half private home: the seaside
  commercial wings are provided with second-story
balconies; while the domestic
quarters, colorless annex to vacationers'
  charming hostels, are boarded shut—
    a cast-iron latch fastened
      over each close-fitting set
        of stout cedar shutters. Near the hilltop's
        uppermost strata,
      a posh *Ryokan* abuts—
    elegant tile-roofed verandahs

at each floor level. The inn's base, on a downslant,
　　slopes across a stratified
cliffscape of terraced gardens, four stories
　　visible on one side, six on the other,
　　　　perhaps two or three
　　　　　　underground levels to house
　　　　　　　　the hotel staff: quarters for maidservants,
　　　　　　　　　landscape artisans,
　　　　　　　　　chauffeurs, aristocrat geishas. . . .
　　　　　　Scanning the whole hillside—
　　　　from top to bottom—my eyes suddenly bypass
　　the eclectic diversity
of abodes: I exult in a common glory,
　　shared by one and all—the panorama of roof-
　　　　tiles! A rainbow mosaic
　　　　　　of countless shades and colors,
　　　　　　　　the design or pattern wavering as sun shifts,
　　　　　　　　　darks and lights vary
　　　　　　with the fluctuation of cloud
　　　　　masses, dimming or blocking
　　　　the sun, by turns. At a given moment
　　（as a succession of frames
in a color film of the roofs we still view
　　today quickly reveals), one variegated
　　　　scattering of tiles—which cuts
　　　　　　across many roofs and catches sun
　　　　　　　　at a sharp angle—softly heightens the colors,
　　　　　　　　　producing a foreground
　　　　　　of brightly glinted shapes.
　　　　　Animal episodes. Flower
　　　　bouquets. Human profiles not unlike faces
　　glimpsed in the clouds. . . . Or the eye
swerves to the background gestalt of tiles shaded
　　by the sun's obliquest angle, undertones
　　　　of muted colors—diamonds
　　　　　　and tiny parallelogram flecks
　　　　　　　　shuffled and reshuffled in a swift unfolding
　　　　　　　　　of suaver images,
　　　　　　　　but no less vivid a flux
　　　　　　　of emblematic portraits from life. . . .
　　　　Or, in moments of idle witnessing, the eye
　　fumbles—a blinding flash drowns
all color in glare! A mirror-sheen of tiles—

few in number but fatal in brilliance—
    reflects the light, blazingly.
        It coerces the viewer to blink,
           or glance to one side. . . . Our film captures
           each configuration
        of the shifting tableau's
    alchemy, in turn. I find,
    if I slow to a halt the flow of celluloid
    through the projector, I may catch—
in blurred frames—the rare moment! All three tile
    mosaics spring into view, at once, coincide,
        and form a montage: each figure
        glows in an independent plane,
           claiming its own distinct niche in the spectrum
           of visible light;
           the display of colors—in each—
        projects a dominant hue,
        or nuance, set off from the others; yet they merge
    and blend in one composite,
the ghostly flux of the movie screen. Now one
    appears to leap closer to the viewer—
        while two figures recede—
        now another, the mobile field
           of tiles passing through the two stationary
           planes, in each advance
        and retreat. Interplay, or clash,
        between the varicolored tableaus—
    a triptych montage—reveals the unearthly beauty
    of this hillside township
as in a timeless, fourth dimension. . . . Today,
    our film commences, anew, to uncoil
        from its slender reel taking
        us back five years to the hour
           we first stood on the broad mesa, and viewed
           Kashikojima's
        brilliant festival of roofs:
        the indigent cottages
    and huts, frugal chalets (twin *Minshiku*), posh
imperial villas
and drab offices—all sporting, in concert,
    ski-sloped roofs, overhanging eaves curving
        upwards. . . . *Hands of a troop*

of subaltern gods reaching out
  to catch the rain, fingers upcurled to embrace
    whatever manna falls
  from skies perpetually charmed
by the visual Mardi Gras
of tile displays checkering the unbroken sweep
of circular landscape,
tiles of all shades glittering around and around,
  alike in pale sunset pastels, halftones;
    midday sheens of gold;
      or morning riot of greens, blues,
        reds—bold wholetones: a hillside cornucopia
          of color ablaze!

THE TILEMAKER'S HILL FRESCO

1.

The veteran tilesmith,
near his hut beneath the central bluff, cuts deep-dyed tiles
to shape. He salvages
the miscast odd pieces, molded wrongly
by kilns in his tileworks, that makeshift factory:
a few pre-fab steel girders
reinforced with concrete blocks and sealed with mortar;
walls on the north side only, the exposed frame
welcomes tenants—hawk or rodent. . . . Assisted
by one skilled teenager,
he bakes thousands of fired-clay tablets daily. Together, they lift

the many glazed flat slabs
piled in neatly proportioned, truncated pyramids, stacked
high—but without a wobble—
in the two black wheelbarrows and rolled,
swiftly, to the tailgate of a fifties Ford pickup.
The two symmetrical heaps
of tiles are slid, intact, on a tough woven fabric, then
eased onto a mobile platform in the truck back—
a hydraulic jack?—which lifts or lowers
great bulks to the desired
level. The double load, transported across a steep upgrade

to a nearby hilltop
temple, is raised on the hydraulic device to a broad-based
scaffolding of ropes and boards.
The youth wrestles lines in the difficult
pulleys, while his mentor guides the plank framework:
now both tug the stage underfoot,
winding the combined weight of persons and two loads
of tiles, in slow—but constant—lift to eaves
of the curved high chapel roof. The self-
propelled escalator,
thin platform swinging in place, quits. They fasten the thick ropes,

swift hands weaving graceful
knots and loops, a classic ropecraft! *Tests knots. No slip-*

slack. Back-up knots, made fast
with snap of wrists. Fisherman's cast-reflex.
The tilemaster nods to his co-roofer. He spirals down
the dangling rope-end, unwound,
feeding through his two-fisted grip. *Rope-dancer!*
Or fireman sliding down ice-slick pole, who,
gaining speed as he nears the ground, brakes
just before impact! The man
on the roof crawls skyward, the load of tiles swelling his orange

back-pack: *buffalo's hump*
silhouetted against the bright cloud mass above him. His hilltop roost far higher than ours,
we view him on an upslant: his stooped figure,
crablike, bordered by a shimmer of pinkish light, floats
across the roof's marked incline.
The master, too, looms above us, stretching to full height—
balanced, through shakily, on his truck-cab roof,
parked a short distance from the temple.
He surveys a dozen roofs,
all his own creations (the bounty of his thirty years' tenure—

by exclusive contract—
to the town), scattered, above and below, at graduated
and terraced intervals,
around and around the steep bluff, now topped
by the near-finished temple, appending its rich contour
of crosshatched dormers and gables
flowing between the pinnacle-spire and curled roof eaves
to the township's skyline. A bewitching sweep
of commingled roofs and hill-crests notch
Kashikojima Bay's
coast range. . . . Is that weathercock, or true hawk, crowning the chapel's

spear-tipped steeple? I wonder. . . .
Snuffed out. In a fleeting moment, erased! All outlines,
in this incisive clarity
of light, are clean-cut saliencies: Calder
sheet metal cutouts, hung from invisible thin wires
in a vast outdoors mobile—
improvised, say, to honor a Chicago Civic Center;
the artist concealed, hid behind his Cosmos

like the puppeteer lurking to one side
of marionette strings,
or the elegant tilesmith and roof-architect vanishing, today,

into anonymity
behind their roof tableau, while timber-and-tile highrise
sculptures convert to church,
residence, town hall, hospital, locomotives'
roundhouse, airship hangar and bus terminal. . . . All roofs
take their place in the grand collage
of Japan's countrywide tile mosaic, a coast-to-coast
color kaleidoscope of the roofers' fine art.
Each town and city displays to bird's-eye
or airplane overview
its own uniquely sprawled horizontal roof fresco, shifting tilescapes

remodelled as lodgings fall
and are built again, fashioned by the accidental combined
hands of tilescraft genius. . . .
Now the maestro, thirty-year-veteran,
stretches on tiptoe for the widest panoramic truck-top
vista of his rooftile fresco-
in-progress. He is waving his arms to the apprentice,
scolding directions, guiding the skilled handyman
on the roof through difficult crawls, hobbles:
sporting binoculars (twins
of *our* field glasses), he choreographs a dance of tile jugglery. . . .

2.

Impresario of the hill,
the happy tile-czar plots and maps out his roofdancer's
intricate moves. A pattern
unfolds. As the master prompts, so the protégé
lays tiles. Then, he breaks new ground: when he takes risks,
flouts rules, his eyes glow! Choices,
choices abound. Hazards of spacing, color arrangements,
placement of off-shade tiles of varied shapes
and odd sizes: triangles, diamonds, ellipses,
rhomboids, squares perhaps—
he rejects false settings, color match-ups that do not ring true

for his keen tilist eye.
He selects—in the speedy flux of options—happiest
blends and designs. Journeyman
and fledgling, bowed to his knees, he still tracks
signals from his tutor by taking quick sidelong glimpses—
ah, slowly he creeps into his roof-
walker's second skin of an artist!
                           The coach on the truck-top
devises a code as diverse (to our untutored
eyes) as semaphore alphabets—if delivered
flagless, batonless. *Forearm*
hand chops. Airbursts of cupped-hand poppings in underarms. Curled tongue

clickety clacks. Forehead thwacks.
Castanetlike finger-snappings. . . .
                           Light shifts. The tilemaster,
elongated in stark relief
against the hillside backdrop, casts a long shadow
which seems to quiver, magically, in the lusterless sheen
of the late dull sun. The shadow,
undulant, wavers from side to side, flickering upon walls
of three or four of the nearby buildings, all roofed
by his own tile handiwork over the years.
His shadow fluctuates, now,
in rhythm with the encroaching dusk wind's soft hands giving caress

to the flat cedar sidings
and broad wall panels. So intensely does he behold (his eye
a camera's wideangled lens),
he takes in a one-hundred-eighty-degree expanse,
a topography of roofs mantling the hill, at all levels
from summit to ground zero. . . .
We sense the pace of teamwork quickens, accelerates, both men
racing the fall of the sun, and the last good light
does seem to falter, to stall, as if secretly
befriending their labors
(oh, beauteous enterprise!). . . .
                           It may be, the master exults: a trance

steals over his features,
while he scans the exquisite geometries of his hillslope
mosaic nearing completion.
The bluff looks subdivided, carved by late shadows

and oblique slants of light into three wide tall panels
of a vast outdoors triptych
facing to east, north, and west. He rotates his binoculars,
slowly, from side to side, bowing his head in homage,
thrice, to each phantasmal scarp of tile-roofed
declivity. Each roofshelf,
a distinct plane of hillscape, expresses—in its pattern of shuffled

blocks, plates, and flat oblongs
of color stacked like bright dominoes in sloped-roof chains—
a range of tones to match Nature
herself. The scene beheld offers to our eyes
a new calculus for decoding Planet Earth's minute lush
particularity, which,
if viewed by a Paul Cézanne, say, could reveal—in a flash—
a first Incarnate Alphabet for Cubist art. . . .
Taking turns with *our* glasses, we oscillate
between tiers of tile layouts—
unevenly spaced, at many sites of hillside—and rainbow terraces

of nearby flower gardens
fashioned by local experts in Ikebana, arrangements
of azaleas, peonies, irises,
camellias and morning glories, clustered
in bright patches on the hillface—zoned in geometric
segments: long narrow rectangles,
wide ellipses, isosceles triangles, squares, trapezoids,
each a rioting cornucopia of color
mirroring the palette (limitless
shades, tones, hues, nuances)
of adjacent tile displays. Here, the tranced viewer grasps images

of the seen world as a flux
of intersecting cones, rotating cylinders, pyramids, cubes
and spheres. All living parts
of *this* landscape, to be deciphered by human eyes,
must be apprehended as a pattern of colors and shapes
molded by joint artistries
of the Ikebana horticulturist and rooftile architect
(the two cultures, with unearthly charm, nourish
each other, casting a double spell
on haunted witnesses):
the Eye, thus illumined, dissects Nature into a mesh, webwork

of geometric solids,
whirling like pinwheels or weathervanes in juxtaposed orbits.
Sight, itself, takes the form
of so many diamonds and spheroids, revolving
in the perfect balance of gyroscopes, planets, asteroids!
They are both the scene beheld
and the Eye's imitation of it. The myriad-flecked
tile-and-flower show and the act of seeing
are One. Cubism. Not a concocted pose,
dogma of elitist few
savants, but true faculty shared by the Eye and all things sighted.

3.

I fancy the tilemaster
in his youth—devotee of Cézanne's landscapes, his passion
burgeoning throughout six years
of study and travel in France. Today, finding
in terrains of his homeland prototypes for the exalted
hidden orders rendered
luminous, as by fluoroscopy, in Cézanne's great cliff-scarps
in oils, he sets out to electrify for common eyes
(and ours!) the extraterrestrial beauty
of unseen geographies
lurking within many a haunted landscape. This seaside bluff is the last

tableau of his secret career
in alchemy, his mission as translator of the actual earth,
terrestrium on the city's
outskirts, into its ideal other form: *divine roof-
symmetries!* . . . By following a mathematics of tile layouts
wedding Nature to homecrafts,
a celestial earth dweller's art, he does honor to both
Pythagoras' "Music of the Spheres" and Lucretius'
De Rerum Natura, but taking Cézanne
as his patron Saint. . . .
Now he infuses into body language of his delivery hand-wafts

of dance choreographer,
lilted gestures of band conductor on his podium, or opera
scenarist molding stage sets
(he has studied their styles in theatre rehearsals). . . .
So it is he waves commands to his apprentice and heir,

the disciple who may carry
into the future this rare exterior decorator's genre
of landscapist high art. . . .
                              The low ochre sun,
passing behind a slow cloud, reemerges,
                    darkening to wine-amber
as it nears the horizon. All the petal-and-tile bouquets take on

            shades of crimson, lowest tiers
        incarnadined, the highest cloud-pale pinks. The men, as before,
        quicken their to-and-fro signals
    and tile settings. The master *is* Cézanne, his canvas
    the many-layered sweep of hillslopes. They rage to finish
  two small dormer roofs by dark,
    cupolas perched, mosquelike, on opposite sides of the base roof
serving as floor to the two miniature domes. The tilists,
wearied, have saved for last, for day's end,
                these exact twin replicas
of the temple structure below, models of the original church

            fashioned to the smaller scale
        in all particulars, two whole tiny chapels atop the parent
        tabernacle. . . .
                              The tall youth,
        stretching to his full lanky height, reaches upwards
        from the lower roof, a steeplejack on his tower stacking
    tiles in immaculate rows,
        then anchoring them in place with steel rivets. Working in clockwise
    circles around each dwarf roof, in turn, he slams the barrel
of his rivet gun into roofboards, vibrating
                the whole midget cabins
in his fury, taking fire from his senior co-aerialist, each balanced

            on his flat roof trapeze:
        the one waltzing in circles, around and around a temple top
        of cracked planks and shaky rafters
        (saved by the stout cedar king posts and ridgepole);
        the other stomping up and down, bobbing on the rust-eaten
    truck roof below, partway caved-in
  on the rearward side, tattered upholstery showing through gaps
  in the metal. Now the superior is waving his arms,
gesticulating in a final passion: last

block-outs of the design
and color match-ups. No time left to correct mistakes, all last choices

of chromatic blends and tile-
fittings are blurted out in a flash of sudden insights, a blaze
of second-seeing, as day's light
slowly fails. . . .
Though the air is still (no leaf or petal
flickers), all garden plots and roofs break up before his eyes!
The separate roof tiles and blooms
lose their outlines—their natural borders, edges, surfaces
and skins blurring. The inner substances, or mass,
spills out of its casings. All things living,
or non-living, transgress
the limits set by orders of chemistry and physics. Thus, the atoms

and molecular bondings
of each flower species; the compounds of each scent, fragrance;
the meshwork of electrons
in each element of metals, rocks, earth clods, seabrine
and mountain streams—all are breaking up in the cyclotron
of the artist's piercing vision.
Laser beams or high-speeding supersonic neutrons of second sight
bombard all things, exploding their atomic make-up,
dissolving their nature, a Second Nature
welling up from wreckage,
the ruins of matter. A new order, phoenixlike, is born from debris.

All souls of flower, rock, soil,
timber, flint, glass, tile—come back as galaxies of perfectly
formed geometric bodies,
symmetrical as snowflakes, spinning in fixed planes
or circling in three-dimensional orbits. Cézanne's spheres,
cubes, and intersecting ellipsoids
project, for the viewer, an order of stable identities.
A mathematics that endures (oh, steadfast cosmos!),
and survives—like inner light—the withering
of vines, stems, limbs to dust . . .
The incincrating of walls, floors, roofs to ash . . . Our collapse of bodies. . . .

THE GRAVE RUBBINGS

(for Laurence Donovan and Dee Clark)

Perched on one
leg, pale egret atop a rock,
arms outstretched
for balance—less bird than scarecrow!—
I hover on the summit of Kashikojima Bluff, and praise
the late, indolent ruddy sun,
squat pomegranate poised over Ago Bay....
The children, long since
drifted off with their mother, meandering
to a downhill plateau—
their zealot voices, echoed in the distant gulch, break
into my reverie....
I scan two or three pine groves
stratified on the downslope
beneath my hilltop ledge, hunting their plaids
and colorful stripes; absently, I
focus nearer, and catch a glimpse of three backs—figures
lying facedown, scattered
on a wide ridge
directly below: they look
so close, spied

through field glasses, I feel as if I can place
the flat of my hand between my son's
shoulder blades (he nearest, stationed
just under my lookout—I lean and sway,
neck stretched over the mesa edge for the view)....

Each child, prone
to a flat slab, limbs sprawled
in various postures:
the boy leaning on one elbow,
one of the girls supported, tripodlike, on left knee, left
elbow and right sneaker sole,
she swings her free arm from side to side,
a stroking motion—
all three children are kneading
(with some tool or other?)

on the rough surface under their legs and thighs. . . . I proceed
down the path
advancing toward them, keeping
the glasses focussed
on their labors, noting—in semiprofile—
they straddle wide sheets of paper,
no foolscap but firm-textured quality leaves of drafting bond
begged and secured from Mom's
favorite sketchbook,
black handprint smudges on Isaac's
chin and temple,

long smear across his forehead—telltale splotches!
They wield soft sticks of charcoal, brittle
and crumbly, black flakes of Carla's stub
of snapped char-stick spotting her skirt-
hem like soot, or dye, small chunks flying away

from her clenched
hand as she scrawls . . . *bits*
of hard ash spat
from embers, or hickory coals
ablaze. . . . They cannot be sketching freehand likenesses
of local flora, game
or wildlife, since they never raise their eyes
to check out a model,
nor take the measure or scale
of a subject. Strokes—
drudgelike!—are drawn in a to-and-fro plodding rhythm.
Long sweeping lines.
No pauses for accuracy or sharpness
of detail. Pressure
constant, tempo unvaried, their brusque moves
a motion of polishing or sandpaper
scraping—more the act of one smoothing rough surface
than suave strokes of Creator
of Life Studies.
Semicircular wavings. Systole.
Diastole.

The heartbeat of windshield wipers. Oh, my angels,
my creative brood! At last, I pop
the question. "Rubbings, Dad," in chorus

comes the reply. "We're doing rubbings
of tombstone art, story-pictures of local sights. . . ."

I survey
the wide oval cliff-recess:
half of the chosen
acreage, city-zoned, is hidden
under cliff-overhang; the other half a wide plateau-ledge
visible from my former lookout
vantage, above; outer limits marked by two
high red Torii gates,
towering in front and rear, shaped—
I always fancy!—
like colossal models of the Greek letter *pi*. This haven,
adorned with scattered
statuary, is less a graveyard
than open-air museum,
the handful of headstones memorial sculptures—
a few, statues of civic heroes
or saints in local town history. The stone monuments comprise
two pentagons, one octagon, three
wavy ellipses curled
like Calder mobile hangings,
any number

of long rectangles, a few upended to heights
of ten or twelve feet, most lying flat;
two towering figure Ls; one Mitsubishi emblem: three triangles spaced
in a circle, each triangular concrete block

welded to the two
others by lengths of steel tubing;
one high pyramid
perhaps at dead center of the grounds:
the two-dozen-odd steps to the top shelf, thick slabs
of concrete, are graduated in size
from twenty-foot-square base to platform apex
affording footroom
(with little space to spare!) for two
of my junior clan
who, having raced each other to the peak from opposite sides,
are now pushing

and shoving in a king-of-the-castle
contest. Each, claiming
sole possession of the castle keep, tries
to drive the other from the tower
fortress. Scaling the pyramid steps before I can devise
apt verbal threats to fit
the occasion's hazard,
I descend, two turncoats clasped
by scruff of neck. . . .

Older sister, aloof from ruffianly sibling
squabbles, persists in her rubbings,
crowding into a single wide sheet
of drawing paper a carnival
of images transcribed from many tombstones,

in succession.
A wiry she-goat scuttling
on all fours
across the flat-topped octagon, she hops
from one to another of three conjoined Mitsubishi triangles,
winding around the rim of an S-
shaped ellipse; now balancing on the narrow base
of an L, arms
and abdomen draped around the edge
of tall L-throneback.
Scouting for rare finds, she fills the curled page margins
with exact replicas
of script *hiragana* and *katakana*,
Japanese alphabets,
each a handsomely detailed total portrait
in its own right, much curlicued,
derived from Chinese ideograms. The perimeters of her page
are neatly crammed (she ever
the orderly child,
obsessed by tidiness to a fault?)
with lined-up rows

of characters—each coupling two or more pictures
into a single alphabet. The page
corners and foot-wide borders are stamped
with large line drawings of local shrines,
historic belfry, pagoda, and temple buildings,

a few sites
instantly recalled from our one *unguided*
quick tour through town,
the upright originals we'd passed
much simplified in the few lines and spare markings of grave-
stone embossments. . . . Now she moves
by design—as if following a charted itinerary
through hallowed grounds
of the classic dead heroes and ancestors—
to the tallest rectangle.
Holding her work-in-progress up high against erect marble
with one hand—
palm pressed flat, she starts marking
and shading with the other.
Tranced, she works over a large raised portrait
jutting out from the surface—embossed
to thicknesses of a half-inch, or more, details textured,
acute (or so I discern, standing behind
the budding portraitist—
not making a sound, but peering
over her shoulder). . . .

Eyes luminous, she is filling out a large center-
piece of her canvas, the empty space—
a wide circle she left in the middle—saved
for a select masterwork; many smaller
rubbings distributed around the vacancy, a few

squeezed so close
edges touch, or corners overlap.
Alert to audience,
she slows her pace, finds means
to control the balance of lights and darks in her shading,
holding the full length of char-stick
sidewise—flat to the page—for lightening. She marks
with short quick sweeps
of the chalk's blunt end, etching
succinct dots and stripes
free of fuzzy smears. She is developing style, a fine art
of rubbings! But the spiel
she gabbles to her eavesdropper parent—
palaver of truisms—dissects

expertise at rubbings, as if she'd foreknown
the whole repertory of skills.
Yet I can read the glut of discovery in her eyes: surprises
of touch, her fingertips' supple finds—
sensory illuminings!
Response to sudden caprices
of medium. Flarings-

out of a new intelligence gushing into handprint
whorls, wrist-reflexes, fingerjoints:
a chalk flattened against digit knuckles
slides into wispier flourishes (arcs
and swirls that adorn light shadings) than finger-

ends afford;
extended index finger guiding
long line-sweeps
better than leading thumb.
This miracle of mating handrhythms to medium is *her being* now,
this new artifice she rolls
and slicks over the page. *The moves starting up*
from her hip and spine
as she dances flowing brush-strokes
of the soft powder-stick
into the midsection of granite. Or shoulder-floats and dips
her down-stroke
into the solar plexus of limestone.
Or hip-swivels and grinds
her side-winding cross-stroke into lumbar vertebrae
of a little rich marble column,
with only the flat thin sheet of wood pulp epidermis gliding
between her pale smooth skin
and coarse-hewn rough
stone skins of the lurking beneath
grand dead,

their bodies' last gristle and integument sighing
back to half-breath in her sneeze primed
by wind-blown black chalkdust snuff
or tickly pollen. . . . No way did a father's
gift, last birthday, of rudimentary homearts paint

kit prepare her
for outdoorsarts of tombstone
massage and rubdown:
"No talent, and no art, Dad. That no-win
toy. . . ." Dimestore number-map paintings. Rote sloppings-on
of pigments. You follow strict equatings
of number-blocks to prescribed colors. No color
blends allowed. Fit numbers
to colors, colors to numbers. Pat
match-ups, all. . . .
Her secret. She lifts her eyes, often, as if seeking hints
for this scenic rubbing
beyond the high squared limestone death
tablet she labors over,
and beyond, even, this cliff-ledge graveyard
(part recessed tabernacle, part
broad mesa)—a distant reference point to which she returns,
again and again, as to touchstone
for testing details
of the incomplete rubbing: a rock-
studded seascape

(the exact contents of the scene eluding me,
prior to this moment—now the broad
outline emerges intact, at last!) . . . .
She tries to hide her stolen glimpses,
furtive. *Tossing her long bangs out of her eyes?*

Or easing a neck-
quirk? But these gestures are faked.
I can decipher her far-
to-near pattern of squints:
following each half-veiled stare in the distance, she reworks
hairsbreadth fine details of wrought
charcoal. . . . So I study the scene portrayed,
both familiar and strange—
it depicts a classic sunrise at sea,
the sun's opulence
wedging a cleft between two huge whaleback-shaped rocks
closely juxtaposed,
a narrow strait, or channel, flowing
between them. The true sun—
at this moment setting behind us—casts

an ashy vermilion glow
over the many sky-piercing memorial stones, silhouetted
on sea and cliff-backdrop.
She never looks back
over her shoulder, whether to glare
at the parent-spy

crowding her easel-stance and blocking the last light,
or to steal views of the broad prospect
of sunset on the opalescent sea-tract
at our backs. No model of the sun
(in ascent *or* descent) having caught her eye, I search

the anterior skyline
horizon for images, images to match
her secret borrowings
and glosses on the original *text*
of the nature-study in raised relief on the tall stone's face. . . .
Ah, beautiful thieveries! The wedded
rocks of Futami spring into view, just visible
above the high left scarp
overhead —lurking a little outside
my line of vision
while I hung suspended, fluttering over the able draughtswoman's
locks. Now, stooping
to inspect minute details of her craft,
I find myself sharing
a far corner of her perspective, the stark view
of Futami dodging into my vista.
I follow the long thick straw rope across its hammocklike swoop
and suspension from a topmost front edge
of the high rock-island's
slanted cone to the egg-shaped crag
of the lower isle,

and I insert a mental picture of the famous sunrise,
the squash-colored vast disc passing upwards
between the rocks, filling the cleavage
(cork stopper in bottle top), as in Carla's
near-to-finished rubbing of Futami. *The top arc*

of fireball
in ascension is stalled parallel

to a wooden Torii's foot—
the great tall pi-*shaped cypress tower*
anchored to the large island's peak, lording its full height
over the sun in stasis of art's deep-
freeze. The slack straw rope, bisecting the solar
orb (a drooped ring
of Saturn?), marries Futami's two rocks;
the tattered annual yoke
replaced with great ceremony each January 5, those rock-island
mates symbols
of Japan's two mythic creators—
Izanagi and Izanami. . . .
How well she knows she improves on the engraver's
handiwork! Hurrying now, she races
the dimming light, conserves the last sun strong enough to work by
(mirroring the mind of the scene
portrayed, she'd freeze
Sol dead in his celestial tracks
for the half-hour

it may take her to finish). . . . Now adding frayed straggle-
ends to the rope, and daubing traces of halo
aura to the rock-island crowns, she conjures up
flickerings of the haunted presences
of myth trapped incarnate in the sea-whipped rocks. . . .

III. RUNAWAYS

DOMINICAN SHOE TINKERS

One narrow doorway: five small figures,
   silhouetted in glare light
of the hot midday sun—
    ranging from four
to three feet in height—come hopping,
lopsidedly,
      into the long room. Each child
      totes a sawed-off,
heavy contraption of boards
hung by a shoulder

strap and bouncing on his hip in time
   with his off-center hobble. . . .
All seem to appear at once,
   but no more than one
bulky entrepreneur—at a time—can fit
through the door.
      Four to ten years old, we'd guess!
      Each boy hoists
his unwieldy box—combined
shoesmith's anvil,

toolkit and stool—with a unique lift
   and carry. One by one, they scout
past our table, exhibiting
   their wares. Each stoops
to inspect our boots and sandals—
rattles off
      agendas of defects in shoe-
      handicrafter's
lingo, offers repairs and shine.
Itinerant boot

tinkers, they pursue tourists and locals,
   alike, at all hours. . . . One junior
foot scholar and shoe healer,
   the shortest elf,
spins a yarn of woe: certain heel-and-toe
disasters, foot

twists, ankle spasms, arch cave-ins;
    toe arthritis,
Achilles' tendinitis—if repairs
are delayed or botched.

Our eyes meet. Agree! We'll entrust our feet
    to this small tradesman-artisan.
Propped on his low stool, or
    squatting on his hams
beneath our circular one-piece dining
table, he works
    his tools as we ours: chisels,
    cuts and shaves sole
leather; batters nails with a ball-peen
tapper into heel

Neolite, while I saw scraps of sheep flesh
    from nubs and tubes of bone, or stab
smallest morsels with knife tip
    or fork tine prong,
you trapping rice flecks between chopsticks
flashing like blades
    of a scissors. The urchin
    below our plates—
so small of carriage—sits upright
as he glues and rips,

sews and taps, not hunching his shoulders
    or bowing his head—an inch or two
safe clearance between his scalp
    and the oak slab
undersides. Our four legs straddle
his hacked seat,
    which he swivels from side to side,
    fluttery. As he works,
he pivots, taking turns with your feet,
mine, stroking your limbs

perhaps, while he fits the shoehorn tongue
    in and out—he finds a relish, a joy,
in sliding our shoes off
    and on, many times,

chanting and humming as he scrapes
and gouges. . . .
    He peers, often, between our legs,
    extending his close-
shaved head, tortoiselike, stretching
his neck (too far,

it seems), inviting our tips on detail,
  but more to flirt with his sparkly
brown eyes than to consult—I
  whisper in your ear,
between bites. You suppress bursts
of laughter
    disguised as fake swallows, hiccups,
    his tiny fingers
flitting about your ankles, legs,
tickly to bare calves

and lower thighs. . . . He slicks the waxy gunk
  and paste thick on shoe tops and toes
for the shine. Saddle soap
  lather trickles
and foams down your leg. You gurgle
on a huge gulp
    of beer, and upset the half-full
    El Presidente
bottle. I yank my plate to one side,
splattering blots

of curry sauce on bare table top, your dress,
  my cotton pantleg, brown stains
flowing across the cracks
  in board oak. . . .
The non-union scab strikebreaker erupts
from his workbench
    roost as Cupid from sea surf,
    blond curls awash
in beer foam, yellow-orange streaks
running down his neck.

Oblivious to the unique swirls and whorls
  of his make-up, his face and neck

a canvas displaying new modes
   of expressionist
culinary spatter art, he now cups
our shoe bottoms—
     first yours, then mine—in his proud
     hands. *Finito!* . . .
Splendid shine. Muy pronto, we lie,
paying up. . . .

EROS AT THE WORLD KITE PAGEANT

(Santiago, Dominican Republic)

Our host, Don Tomás Morel—retired mayor,
    poet, folklorist—slips off
        into nostalgias. . . . He takes us back
            fifteen years
            to the earliest days
    of his seclusion—
        the withdrawal from public
office, his shy first trials and delights
    as amateur folklorist,
            the slow nurturing of his zeal
    to revive the lost communal folk arts—fad
        of his youth. . . . Ah, he begins
        with kites. First, a scholar, he researches

            the origins of kitecraft
        in ancient tribes, poring over old sketches,
            rudimentary drawings
    of virtuoso kites;
            then, he molds large block
                prints portraying fantasy kites
            in designs that recall Marc Chagall's dream flights,
                and runs off hundreds of colorful posters
        highlighting the date, place, and prizes
        to be awarded in the first worldwide kite contest. . . .
    Each week, for two months,
        drafting new kite models, he despatches
        couriers to all seaside cities, mountain or backwoods
    towns, to hang the posters on all prominent
    billboards, roadside barns,

and farmers' markets—promoting the all-star
    kite Olympiad. He sponsors
        bi-weekly ads on radio and T.V.
            news broadcasts
            for all the world as if kite-
        flying pageants,
        or tourneys, are as common
    as annual lotteries, beauty queen contests,

or cockfights. . . . The weekend
   of kitefest, whole townships come
  to Santiago from all parishes of the country
   in caravans mixing ox-carts,
    motorbikes, schoolbuses, horsemen, firetrucks,

    twenty-wheel semi oil rigs,
   chauffeur-driven Rolls limos, two-cylinder
    electric cars—record traffic
  jams on all main roads
    into town, many families
     pitching tents and slinging hammocks
    between trees eight to ten miles outside the city
     limits (to avoid the "criminal riffraff"). . . .
  At daybreak, a full hour before sunrise,
   hundreds of men and boys assemble at the foot
  of the one hogback-
   humped broad high hill in town, topped
   by Trujillo's columnar tower—one of many monuments
scattered about the country his worship erected
to commemorate himself

in a race, perhaps, with his own assassin.
  Most kite-makers tote two
   or more kites, cradled away from raw wind-
    chops, the delicate
   glossy papers and silks tied
  to featherweight
  thin sticks of balsam: all kites
are wrapped in bed sheets or heavy-gauge plastic
  (so like prize fighting-cocks
   shaded under hoods and carried
   to the bout in cages). . . . Each lone kitist climbs
   to his appointed hillside
   terrace. The three or four dozen acres

   of grassy slopes encircling
  the monument are subdivided and parceled out
   to all registered entrants,
  while the plateau
   on the hill's far side—

a treeless expanse groomed and trimmed
yearlong as a polo grounds—is reserved for hundreds
of teenage and child kitists, who are allotted
half-hour shifts, from first light to dusk.
Today, even the "Capuchin," the tiny-to-small kites
of the children, are dubbed—
with strict formality—*flying artifacts.*
But early on, the kids may be seen racing to and fro,
crisscrossing, tripping over each other's lines,
falling and laughing

and colliding with their fellows, from one end
of the polo courts to the other.
One child, ignoring the shouts and appeals
of thousands
in the clumped galleries
of spectators,
continues to chase a runaway
kite trailing a swiftly unwound ball of string,
his legs entangled
in three or four lines issuing
from opposite directions—now dragging two dropped
and bedraggled spools of twine,
as well as the downed kite of a comrade

twisting and shredding on the turf
in his wake. Another tall kite, descending, swoops
onto his back like a vulture,
its upper brace of crossed
sticks clinging to his shoulder,
two strips of white sheeting dangled
from his spine as he runs, a white devil's forked tail. . . .
The two judges in pursuit are retired police
sergeants: one thick-necked and hippy,
the other preceded by a colossal triple chin
billowing into tight-
belted double paunch, the latter resembling
an upright camel's twin humps. As if he carries sacks
of molasses, his multiple jelly rolls of flesh—
bouncing up and down

as he runs—keep up their own unique tempo
of jiggles and jolts, queerly

at odds with the rhythm of his galloping legs
and erect frame.
Red-faced, he bellows threats
at the fugitive:
"Rule-breaker, you're disqualified!
Halt! Pay the fines," all lost on those runaway
urchin ears. But most infant
kite-flyers abide by the rules,
staying within the time limits and narrow borders
of their allotted purlieu
on the polo turf. The nearsighted, half-deaf

judges, milling around the junior
contestants, mark points on their bulky pasteboard
scorecards, catching kite-tails
and snagging slack lines
in their stiff formal uniforms,
defaulting more often than any child:
they back into each other, signposts, and out-of-bounds
markers, as they weave in and out of the ranks
of four or five youth divisions
bunched, by age increments, in far corners of the field....
One skilled operator,
juggling two kites of Punch and Judy—
one set of strings in each hand—employs a precise code
of finger controls, giving to the airborne
hero and heroine

animated and sprightly stick-figure moves
of marionettes. All limbs
and face parts (lower jaw, ears and nose)
wag, or gesture,
independently in the vivid
sky pantomime,
both puppet figures launched
into sudden jumps, dives, side-leaps and bouts
in the celebrated
love-spat battles of the sexes.
The slaps and falls are tautly measured, despite gusts
and sudden shifts in wind direction,
the wind a quick-change artist in its own right

matched, swerve for swerve, by this child
prodigy puppeteer. . . . The fans and other performers,
    diverted from their antics,
are swept away
        by the mime show's last act,
            a spellbinder! Punch clobbers Judy
into a terrific nosedive and tailspin. He zooms
        after her in pursuit, overtakes her plunge
but—unable to stop—Punch hurtles
    toward earth, his pointy nose aimed at a mesmerized chaplain-
judge's unprotected
        bald pate. Ah, it's Judy who loops,
        at the last, and breaks Punch's deadfall, catching him
in a fluttery kite-twinning hug and kiss,
    the two figures sailing off

in separate leisurely ascents. . . . No one doubts
    the verdict: winner of the Junior
League first prize. The senior competition gets off
        to a slow start,
        many distinguished entrants
arriving late, drunk;
    the main events in full swing by mid-
afternoon, perhaps eight hundred of the expected
    two thousand artifacts
        in the "Chichigua" (maxikites)
    division crowding the lower heavens with dense kite
        galaxies and constellations,
        amazingly few sideswipes, tangles, or snarls,

        in view of the congested
    sky field. At peak overcrowding, swarms of kites
        of all sizes and shapes
    dodge each other
            in high winds, the flat kites
                limited to diagonal and up-down
            trajectories, a few tall box-kites spiralling
                and looping in horizontal orbits. . . .
    Someone exclaims, Trujillo's monument
    should be employed—by judges who are not half-blind—
as an airport watchtower,

controllers allocating the throngs
    of airtraffic to restricted sky lanes. . . . Now the veteran
  kite-flyers, leaping hurdles, migrate up and down
  the various strata

of hillside, swiftly traversing the short arcs
    of Government Hill's perimeter
      ascribed to their maneuvers. They keep seeking
        better vantage
        to display their aerial stunts
      and handicraft
      to the audience and judges,
  alike, thousands of spectators merging in clusters,
    here and there, at the hill's
          foot (the viewers roped off from rugged
        hillslopes, reserved for kite pilots). . . . When a new star
          brightens the firmament of kites,
          news travels fast through the clumped masses,

        and a great surge of thousands—
      leaving a few lost stragglers all but trampled
        underfoot in the wake
    of the stampede—
          sweeps to the rumored site, to get
            close-up views of particular marvels. . . .
        The flying *El Presidente* beerbottle starts to sputter!
          Its top blows off with a great pop, an explosion
    of many fireworks at once—the smoke
      billows gushing from the bottleneck stimulate the head
  on a fizzly giant glass
      of beer. . . . No sooner do the vast wings
      of the crowd on the hill's east side converge into one
  shouting and swaying and heaving crush of fans,
  the next aerial highlight—

punctual as Halley's Comet—flares into view
    at a remote edge of the skyfair
      arena, and a whirling vortex of onlookers
        is swept, helplessly,
        into the ideal observatory
      site (as tens
      of thousands of iron filings

are drawn from all sides to a powerful magnet
  suddenly dropped in their midst);
      and now, they charge around the plaza
   to the hill's north end to view, in succession,
     a three-ring-circus staged
    by gifted brothers of the same family

     team, whose renowned surname
  is linked, in memory, to record-setting feats
    in many popular sports.
The spirit invoked
    in the gallery recalls
      blood lust of devotees for a family
   of trapeze artists who perform daredevil stunts
     without a net. The first wields a box-kite
modelled after a flying cigarette
  carton with his left hand, a tall vertical-box lighter
balanced from his right wrist.
  The two boxes float toward each other
   at a height of one hundred meters. The wide carton
box-top flies open—a white giant cigarette
pops out, the lighter top

snapping open at the same instant. A fireworks
  display erupts from the latter,
    igniting the white tip of the giant
     tobacco stick,
     suspended in flight invisibly—
   by its own guideline.
The lit end of the mock cigarette
glows with a dull pinkish gleam (barely sighted
  on the bright sunny backdrop);
    and the slow-burn ember travels,
     by eerie gradual shifts, from one end of the poised
    unmoving white cylinder
   to the other, leaving a scroll of dark ash

    in its place, which disintegrates—
  all at once—into a spray of grey confetti mixed
    with fading sparkles.
The second brother

launches a tall pleated kite,
    much wider at the top than the bottom.
  The many vertical folds, creases running lengthwise,
    resemble a closed accordion's deflated
wind bag. Ah, the pleats commence to open!
The crowd sucks in its breath and gasps, as if they expect—
at any moment—a few chords
  of arpeggios and musical scales
  will come raining down into their ears, a kite concert
of the skies (a fantasy not unlike cartoon angels,
hidden in clouds, plucking

the strings of their small beneficent harps);
  and they avert their eyes from kite
    to wizard, unwilling to let his tricks or sleights
      escape their sight,
      braced for him to perform feats
  as a long-distance
accordionist. But when they look
again, no music ventriloquism is in progress.
  They behold a giant fan
    opening and closing in the sky,
    much as living sea fans are observed to blossom,
    unblossom, in close-ups
    of underwater films shot from bathysphere

    in Jacques Cousteau sea odysseys. . . .
So allured is the audience by the kite-fan's motions,
    bellowslike—its puffed sides
  breathing in and out
    like angels' lungs—they overlook
      the nimble machinations of brother
      number three, who levitates three oddly compressed kites
    at once. Vaguely female, they resemble
floppy deflated clothes mannikins.
  Not until the trio of shapeless scrawny-bird sisters
rises to a level
  some yards below the respiratory fan
  spreading *its* unfolded wing plumes wider and wider—
hypnotic!—do the multitude of viewers lower
their eyes to discover

three dilapidated uprisen women, their flattened
   skin bags starting to fill out,
      swelling faster and faster, while a steady hiss
        (a sound like air
        escaping from a just-punctured
     bike tire going flat:
     or the sound of a manned fleet
of hot-air balloons passing overhead, a hissing
    to drive tame household dogs
       rabid with unstoppable yelping)
      becomes audible to all stationed directly below,
      and to many a short radius
      removed from that bombsight zero precinct. . . .

      The prolonged hiss climaxes
   in a few soft pops, firecracker reports or cap
     pistol shots. By abrupt shifts,
   almost too quick
      for the unaided eye to follow,
        the drooped figures puff into shapely
       dolls, and next, mellow into living dolls kicking
       a cancan (those few blessed with field
    glasscs, or binoculars, catch nuances
    of the sudden anatomical switch, thc swift two-step
   metamorphoses missed
     by the others). . . . The familiai fan,
     above, drops, partially hiding the dancing girls,
  the chorus flirting and teasing thc viewers
with glimpses of their buxom

cleavage and dimpled thighs, while the broad fan
   alternately exposes and shields
     their sexual glamours, as it opens and closes—
     a chastity guard?—
     in front of the chorus line.
    The wideopen fan
    spans all three beauties
executing their bows, kick-ups and pirouettes
   in perfect formation, half-
      veiled behind their modesty screen
      (the two brothers coordinating the four puppet

kites with uncanny true-to-life
spark and verve); the eyes of beholders

    glazed with lust only flesh-
and-blood disco lovelies or go-go twisters
    should arouse. The sober
ecclesiastics
      (divested of all priestly
        garb, doubling as umpires), titillated
     themselves, are willing to pass over lesser deviltries,
      not fooled by the fandancers' screen.
But their dander is piqued by outright
sodomy—for now, blinding sight, slinking down low, lower,
behind the outspread fan
   taking the shape, at last, of a full semi-
   circle, the viewers can guess the lewd acts simulated
by two reclining figures: the prone chorus girl
humping her supine mate, upswung

legs of the latter reversed, the stroking feet
  of both partners to the supposed act
    visible beyond the rim of the half-moon fan. . . .
     The third figure,
     hanging back, tosses her head
   backward and forward,
   though she faces her coupled
and fornicating chums. Now crouching on her hands
  and knees, she passes
     one hand to and fro between her legs
   faster and faster, stopped by howls from the two
   clergymen referees: "For shame!"
   "Foul! Foul!—disqualified. . . ." Louder pops.

    Three beauty queens shrivel,
collapsed in their quick-shrunk hides. The prank backfires.
    Thus, the clear-cut Grand Prize winners,
top-flight family
     talents, are ousted from the weekend
       Olympiad. . . . Three hours to the box-kite
     adult tourneys. Four hours to the bird kites. All winners
     chosen by judges' ballots, the awards given.
The last day's tryouts and contest fêted

by an allout pig and lamb slaughter, followed by allnight
barbecue: whole carcasses
 buried, baked in beds of white-hot coals;
 whole tunas and jewfish flung into the pits, atop the swine:
a fresh-caught gift, gratis, to outland visitors
from the local fisherfolk. . . .

MOONLIGHTERS

Too late for the westend sunset,
stalled on a flat-topped
bluff for hours:
three microbuses
of our caravan parked
at odd angles, we straddle road
and grassy shoulder. . . . Our three
drivers—two Carib Blacks, one East
Indian—squat
beside an aged, tall
pimento tree
(past fruitbearing; bark scrolling off
in long peels; fragrant of allspice, tangy). . . .

They whittle and sand small blocks
and twists of wood into
artifacts,
primitive heads and busts.
Our troop of twenty,
enticed by chanted palaver,
are trapped by a sales force
of dozens, all classes and ages
wielding a sales pitch—
from nonagenarians
to urchins.
The six-year-old oval-faced charmer,
in bermudas, waves colorful cacao bean

necklaces under our flared nostrils,
so freshly picked we whiff
the tart scents
of hacked-open pods. . . .
Men and boys, cane pickers
and huskers, jobless truckers, bauxite
miners and haulers—moonlighters,
one and all! Handicraft experts,
carvers and whittlers,
they offer cut-rate prices
for Afro heads.

[76]

Craggy, wide foreheads. Deep pouches
under eyes. Long sinuous indented ears,

orchidshaped. Carved from coconuts, chunks
of soft cottonwood, guano.
Small handsized
figurines. Totem
pole heads, elongated,
many faces stacked in rows, one
atop the other. Heavy block-
wood sculptures for the mantelpiece.
Basic prototypes—
mythic scowl or dreamy trance—
are repeated
in all sizes. The few artists add
bold flourish to lip or pendulous earlobes. . . .

A teenage boy hands a many-branched
candelabralike limb
through the van
window—we pass the prize
back and forth, driftwood twists
blended with handprint whorl patterns
of the grain (genius in shape
and polishing), the successive branch forks
grafted on all sides
spiralling up the yard-long
stalk, each stem
capped by a removable carved swallow,
thrush, or grackle. The birds, anchored to thin

shafts, are slid in and out of the trunk.
Wide-eyed! That arch of neck
and cast of beak
so lifelike, I expect
wings to flutter, unfurl; tails
to shudder in flight from the hands
of tourists sampling wares,
then fitting the birds back in their sockets
like so many candles
inserted in candelabrum
cups. One branch tip,
someone scolds, is blunted, splintered.
A haggling over prices! This true virtuoso

wood sculpture—marred by one *un*perfect
edge—drops, drops in price
while Voodoo
and Obeah busts command
outsize fees . . . A shuffling of sandaled
feet! The oldest merchant, face
shrunk and furrowed like a prune or fig,
prances in front of a small child
parading necklaces.
He, inches shorter, stunted
and hoop-backed,
struts from side to side, a hop-and-skip
dance step, strumming a makeshift wee violin:

an eight-inch hollow bamboo segment
carved to a miniature
fiddle shape,
the bow a slim turkey
bone wand swept to and fro
across three mounted dental floss strings.
He squeaks forth his repertoire
of catchy tunes, keeping up
a vervy beat. Note-
flawless! *Home on the Range.*
Oh, Susannah.
Old Belafonte calypso hymns. He sells—
crowd humming along—two dozen bows, fiddles. . . .

SALTCOD RED

Curled red locks looped back over the shoe-sole parabola
bald strip indenting your scalp, and fanning out in a bulb

in back; thick cockney accent; eye wrinkles more deeply furrowed
on the left side, left cheek always lifted for the chuckles

or chronic bursts of laughter—your happiest trait—that threads
in and out of your story-telling gabble; fine figure

of a tall man, still the *impress* cut by your lordly swagger
despite round-shouldered stoop and swaybacked cave-in of spine

(lordosis on one side twinned by paunch on the other). . . . You muse
upon the years lost in Foreign Service in the Veldt, worse

in the African Bush—you *bore* your malarial fevers
(no water for days at a stretch), while others in the camp

sank into coma, weekly, you left with seasonal joint aches,
arthritic twinges—no more; and now, even as I whine

my paranoid asides, terrified of machete-armed
Jamaican muggers hiding behind each rock or shrub, you bolt

erect! You add three inches to your six foot sag-frame,
anterior and posterior S-curves flattened into Youth's

ramrod physique reemergent ("No thieving riffraff will dare
to hit on *us!*"), these weeks a well-earned respite from bonanza

years in fresh-frozen fish, back home in frigid Montreal!
Little do the native islanders guess your company

exports tons of Canada saltcod which, coupled with local
ackee redfruit, makes up the favorite national food:

SALTFISH & ACKEE a native emblem displayed in all diners
and speakeasies, alike. I grin at all jokes heard, jokes unheard;

[79]

I must see your profile, half-read those lips to decipher
your rich brogue (lampoonings of all local foibles).... Too shy

to beg you to repeat punch lines, I'm happy to catch tuneful
song lyrics of your badinage if I miss the sly words....

SONG OF THE RIVER SWEEP

(Dunn's River Falls, Jamaica)

1.

Apogee.
The summit. Together, we've climbed,
      rock-tier by tier,
surmounting the last posted milestone
      to a higher overlook—Dunn's River Falls cascading
      in graduated
shelves, light rapids spaced out
      over miles of slopes
terraced beneath our rock-tower vista
      affording, equally, views below and above:
      Seven Rivers—
resplendent!—traversing bluffs
      and rolling foothills
ranged as far as Eye's lassoings
      of visible horizon, the rivers cutting mesas and upper
      plateaus
into near-equal wedges. Commencing
      from diverse latitudes
of the Island's northmost perimeter,
      all seven waterway arteries and tributaries converge
      in the One
Dunn's River passage—an oval bottleneck:
      calm as a lake, transparent,
poised over the plunging column of whitewater
      falls.
      The runoff, below, is abruptly squelched, foam
      levelled
upon scattered boulders. . . .
      Downstream,
      a long human chain, led
by two guides, winds upwards, hands
      claw-curled in a forty-person interlock of unbroken
      links. Chain mates
weave between the breakwater rocks.
      They approach the base
of our lookout. Teetering on the rim,
      you pitch from side to side—a solo samba routine—
      the dance moves

[81]

improvised to match shifting grips
                    on your bulky Yashica
transferred from hip to shoulder, and now,
            arms extended, a two-handed thrust over your head.
                    You reposition
the camera's face for best angles:
                    shooting your wife,
your three fast friends, the linkage of hikers
            and waders threading—by cautious sorties—uphill....
                    Now skirting
the fountainhead of the strongest whitewater
                    falls, they duck and swerve
the last possible instant to miss a dunking
            in churned-up pockets.
                            It is a fencing match of parry
            and thrust
between the pliable string of human sausage links
                    and sudden gushers of foam.
A curling and uncurling bridge of bodies,
            stick-figures fused at arm hinges like clusters of paper
            doll cutouts,
    this conga line-up of tourists gropes—
                    in leapfrog hops—from stone
to underwater stone, often climbing on knees
            over wide flat slabs, hands still clamped to chain pals,
                    fore and aft,
    the skirmishers reeling across the riverbed
                    in an undulatory formation
adjacent to the channel's west shoreline....
            Unseen by the safari of waders, a scattered work force
            of islanders,
many transporting large wooden washbuckets,
                    slowly traverses the downgrade
shallows of the east bank, nearing the leaders
            of the guided upstream hike.
                        The native women, shirtsleeves
            and long pantaloons
rolled to the elbows and knees, pause to exchange
                    whispered gibes, snickers....
So we speculate, peering from our cliff-top refuge
            and observatory: do they not scoff at the host of vacationers
                    in polkadotted
    and beflowered swimwear?...

                              Middle-aged housewives
                         in widebrimmed straw hats,
moonlighters, they are stooping to scrub
                   the overnight moss and filmy sediment from exposed rocks,
                         stepping stones,
            even bottom slates. They scrape off slimes, algae,
                              scums—rubbing all surfaces
with sponge, steel wool and wirebrush, their labor—daily—
                   a race with nature to remove any slick spots. Indeed, they scour
                   the very pebbles
            underfoot, peeling off slippery nocturnal skins:
                              they would restore coarse-grained
surface to all submarine footshelf, or handholds,
                   to insure safe passage. Their diurnal maintenance of hikers' trails
                   ebbs and flows
            in a lilting balletic rhythm, a dance cadence.
                              The river sweep's roundelay. . . .

                                   2.

      Three of the river scrub
crew break up into sport, at once,
      tossing buckets back and forth. Perched
on upraised mounds, they hurl large sponges—squash
            and eggplant shapes—
      at each other's heads, a new mode
      of water polo
      modelled after landlubbers'
      pillow fights. Their upriver fellow
      staffers, an elder
      generation by half, chide
            the horseplay.
         Now the youngish matrons

      play tag: a short obese
walrus, hips wide as two shoulder
      breadths; her three taller associates
high-hipped and bosomy, rolls of waist flab
            rippling around
      all four midriffs. . . . Fleet and agile,
      despite bulk, they wield
      their masses of torsos and backs
      from low rocks to high, as if flesh curves

overlapping curves
are stuffed with excelsior
  or cotton.
      Arms pinned to their sides,

    they logroll their bodies
in sandy shallows, much as lumberjacks
  birl the just-sliced segments of redwood
timbers in Eureka, California:
    all grins and teeth
    whitely flashing, their blubber jostles
    alike in water,
    stone, earth, or spray—at peace
    in flesh is their element, their skins'
    flow continuous
    with the life of surfaces.
      Who can say
        if their happy bodies

    first kiss—or are kissed by—
the foams? More porpoise than mermaid,
  lacking tail of a fish, but backflipping
and sideskipping like dolphins, they arch spine-
      rubber this way
    and that—jointless! Neck, thigh, pelvis
    swim in loose ball
    sockets, unhinged. All skin curves
    are piled upon curves until, fishlike,
    the human hide,
    unforked, is one curved edgeless
        pouch that slides. . . .
        Brown womanlimbs asprawl,

    whatever falls is sun-lifted,
catches itself up like the waterfall
  splashing in their hair and eyes—all falls
playslips, all local fools playwise, sleep swimmers. . . .
      The tourist line-up,
    strung out in a wavery double V, looms
    near. . . . The native crew
    backtrack their rounds, so lightfoot
    and prancy—Zero Mostel's rhino dance!—

retrieved washbuckets
wrist-twirling, in time with jaunty
long river-
slicing strides of their climb. . . .

3.

So absorbed by the fadeout
of the Ocho Rios bucket squad, I miss
the sputtered cries of the chaperoned troop, now fallen,
stooped in tangled
factions of two, three, five—dislodged
from the buddy chain, none smiling, the faces in view piqued
or aghast, a few
dunked in spume of high spray or rapids. . . .

Sampling the dispersed shuffle
of aquatic hikers, hunched or fallen, I try
to guess the cause of the spill, a farcical mishap
that has thrown
all members of the human chainlock
into offlimits flounders, sidcline hobbles and gropings—
as if a demon
underwater prankster has pulled the rug

riverbottom out from under
the scores of catwalking and goose-stepping
folks (a few wearing expressions of aerialists toppled
from a sabotaged
trapeze, irked, doubly, by the absence
of net). . . . I hunt for a familiar frame in the blurred flux
of memory's ceaseless
slideshow, but none fits the unique species

of pandemonium masqueraded
before my eyes. . . . One squatter, favoring a bruised
limb, scans the riverbottom for lost articles: an aged,
princely figure
of a man, a great rolled tuft of white hair
across his back rimming his shoulders like a general's silver
bar decorations
for valor, rivalling the thick Irish moss

density of matted grey piled
　　on his chest, but half-hidden from view as he bends
　　　　from the waist; bending lower, he finally buries his face
　　　　　　in foamy churn
　　　　　　　　of water—he grows too still for comfort,
　　his companion poking him sharply in the ribs to make him raise
　　　　his head, undrowned yet. . . .
　　　　A roly-poly sunburnt Frenchman, fiftiesh,

chases a tri-colored, striped,
　　tall straw hat caught in a whirlpool, spinning down-
　　　　stream (I delight to imagine the midget gymnast, submerged,
　　　　　　who wears the hat—
　　　　　　　　puckish underwater racer, he dances
　　frantic pirouettes: we suppose the hat madly twirls itself). . . .
　　　　The hat's tubby owner,
　　　　hot in pursuit, is tripped—hopping on one foot,

he grasps the other and massages
　　the injured heel, still reaching for the hat,
　　　　which halts, then speeds up as he gropes for the curled peak:
　　　　　　it always jumps,
　　　　　　　　just eluding his outstretched fingers'
　　pinch. A blond teenager, dodging the hat-chaser, gets wedged
　　　　between two rock jaws;
　　　　for a moment, she struggles in panic

as if the rows of stone sawteeth
　　may clamp shut, a live riverbeast's obeah bite.
　　　　Even at this distance, I can make out the angry red welts,
　　　　　　skin embossments
　　　　　　　　risen on both of her exposed upper legs,
　　stings, I surmise, like firecoral lacerations; and now, howls
　　　　from my one warm friend,
　　　　your spunky wife tossing her tomboyish

short bob from side to side. . . . I pivot,
　　turning to warn you to go quickly to her aid
　　　　when I spot your exact twin, below, springing up behind her.

Your camera, left
in haste and still whirring, lies on its side
too near the cliff ledge, dumped, oddly, by that other you my skin
and scalp tell me stands—
if invisible—beside me still, my bones

not confessing your stout skeleton,
escaping, escaped my notice. . . . Puzzled, I lift
the camera and switch off the motor, hoping to salvage
some of the film
left spinning on nothing—a patch of sky!—
by your hasty exit. Now peering into the eyepiece, I adjust
the zoom lens on the scene
below: Marty, horizontal now, is upraised

on the stretcher of your extended arms.
She appears to float on her back, levitating
a foot or two *over* the surface, while a dark fleet figure
approaches with stacks
of gauze bandages (one of the older
washbucket crew, so speedily returned as nurse), who, cradling
heel of the injured foot
in one hand, commences wrapping with the other.

I focus on the wound, the middle
toe capped by a blotch of red where the whole nail
was ripped off. I scan the makeshift hospital ward in midriver,
from east bank
to west, most of the departed scrub force
reprogrammed, spontaneously, as a team of first-aid technicians
armed with tourniquets,
splints (sticks, metal bars), Ace bandages

of all shapes and sizes; chemicals
for swabbing scrapes and cuts (iodine, anti-
biotic creams). . . . Soon, all the fallen viking river-trudgers,
back on their feet
and smiling, join hands and resume
their upriver trek. . . . I linger, fondly, over the paramedical unit,
a last idler, or two,
sashaying a quiet retreat up the east shoreline. . . .

4·

A giantesque
thick-knuckled brown hand,
pointing a direction behind me
and overhead, crosses my lens—
blotting out the scenario below (the pilgrim
explorers, recovered,
boldly heading into the teeth of the falls);
and a lilting voice chants, so close to my ear
I feel the breath on my cheek:
a lesson in geopolitics
and history. . . . I follow the commanding
pointer (hypnotic wand
or baton)—it waves and circles,
tracing the arcs and switchbacks
of each river from its source on the horizon
to its head, or juncture,
with its six mates in the lakesized pool, spread
in unrippled calm above the falls. The hand,
doubled now, blurs: *it is a twenty-*
years-past hand traversing
a ninety-foot-wide many-paneled blackboard,
my anatomy Prof
tracing the webwork of veins
and arteries which converge
in the human heart for a Med student rabble
herded five-hundred-strong
in U. of M.'s colossal amphitheatre. . . .
I'm awed, once more, by Island Earth's body
vessels. Jamaica's rivers!
The wide and narrow alike,
the deep and shallow, the mud-opaque, the crystal
pure transparent: all
conveyors of prime life-support
fluids, life elixirs, they pump
their contents from the many distant river-founts
commencing from seven
widely separate latitudes of sky, funnelled
back to the common basin—the Dunn's River heartpump,
recycling the fetid, stale
lazy-flowing gallon trillions
through sieves and filters of churn-and-churn-about,

purified and flushed
into fields and pastures of harvest,
then rolling into Jamaica's
countless sea-kissed harbors. . . . This forgotten glimpse
of our Body's enchanted
web of rivers, channelled from every distant
limb-terminating cell back to the grand fistsized
pump, the tireless cyclotron
in the left breast, returns in a flash!
My eyes are held by the mentor's hand, my ears
by her throat's warbled
tutelage—in the brief instant
before I drop the camera
to earth, turning to face the long-necked sorceress
sprung up beside me, there's no time
(nor respite in the riverflow of mind) to puzzle
over her unnoticed swift climb from the cliff-base,
by riverside, to my aerial
lookout: she, the senior staff
woman, eldest of the riverbottom unslickers,
slime-removers, scum-
scrapers. Yes, she was the austere head-
mistress of labors I'd beheld
in the rear, chiding her co-workers for their antics.
Then, did she catch glimpses
of the lone hanger-back, outcast or deserter
from the swimsuited gallery, a hillperch snoop
and voyeur? Ah, but taking me
for a student, or learner-aspirant
(armed with pen, scrawled jittery-inked notepad
at the ready), she rose
to my side, unbidden, to steer my eye's
passage and steel my sight
river's meanderings of her particolored country's
many-branched waterways:
streams, channels, creeks, furrows, canals—the whole sweep
of visible outlands webbed and crosshatched
with hairsbreadth fine threads
and rivulets of water. . . . She devotes
her spiel to hand-me-down lore of seven great rivers
conjoined in the Falls,
her sage chatter a hybrid of myth,
family gossip, anecdote,

superstition, legend and true Carib-history
　　delivered in a lingo
blending equal shares of carny-barker's hype, streetsmarts
　　and domestic patter—rhythmed in a lyric cadence
　　　　of poetry. She was a poet
　　　　　　extempore, an improviser
　　　　　　　　of musical phrase, instant yokings of fact and dream:
　　　　　　　　　　a singer of pictures!
　　　　　　　　　　Now hearing I last sojourned
　　　　　　　　in Sister Island Barbados,
　　　　　　　　land of low-lying parched flat acres and drought—
　　　　some parishes so dry,
arid desert compared to her country's lush slopes
　　and vales—she rattles off lists of Jamaica's freshwater
　　　　deep earth bounties. The names
　　　　　　undulate with rolled syllables
　　　　　　　　and liquid vowels proper to bottomless wells
　　　　　　　　　　and unplumbed springs:
　　　　　　　　　　redolent of tall tales she reports,
　　　　　　　　boasts, of record-setting scuba
　　　　and minibathysphere divers boring down, down, down,
　　so many fathoms deep
the partners in science above—hugging the surface
　　but tied to those brave heroes and explorers below
　　　　by a code of tugged ropes,
　　　　　　cables, hoses—lost all touch
　　　　　　　　contact with the oft-reckless scouts of the deep,
　　　　　　　　　　fearing breaks in the line. . . .
　　　　　　　　But the divers resurfaced, always,
　　　　　　　　dizzied and pale, yet resurrected
　　　　　　　in airspace, their vertigo more a spirit malaise
　　　　than the bends, or body
stress. . . . *Oh, what man can abide fathomless depths,*
unscalable heights? . . . Here, the water table,
　　a natural hidden reservoir,
　　　　can be struck anyplace by drills
　　　　　　boring down: this whole country a cornucopia
　　　　　　　　of freshwater springs!
　　　　　　This land a crater-gouged, a miles-long-
　　　　　　drill-shafted . . . Oh, no quarrels
　　　　have I! Squatting, I cup my hand, to scoop up palmed
　　ladlefuls of water
from a mountain spring running past our legs, even

at this height—my small gulps a nonverbal yes. Slurp yes
   to her fervid praise of Jamaica's
      watergods. Slurp yes to oasis fever
         in her eyes. Eyes' glitter signals my hand-to-mouth
           speech strikes home—so I
         sink to all fours, lower my face
      to the stream: lap and quaff great drafts
   of her country's free ambrosias (a mutt in heat stroke). . . .
She, warming to the task,
charts the lineaments of each famed watercourse
   and its tributaries. She hails, in turn, each river
      God's, or Demon's, splendor—
         that amalgam of myth and historic
           peaks. . . . *The Past*

5.

So begins her recitation of high water marks: *El Rio Bueno.*
      A broth of mud-
blackened waters. Mud-opaque. Cows of perennial generations
      of cattle ranches
rim its shores, putrid-smelling thrice-yearly with manure
   and strewn disembowelments, innards of slaughter fouling
      its crusty banks.
      In her thirty-six years of ambles to and from
         Falmouth's

open market, the piquant gallery of cows cheered her twice-
      daily crossovers
of the stagnant Rio Bueno. Wading across the shallow ford
      through drugged currents,
   while she balanced the tall broad wicker basket (empty
      or full) on her cranium, hefting sacks of potatoes
         or bales of feather
           down with equal aplomb and grace, she'd passed
           thousands

of grazing cows, munching riverside sedge and tall grasses.
      Stalled in midpassage,
   her figure motionless like the sluggish waters, she observed—
      with gay painterly eye—
the vivid assortment of shades and colors, a blotched

and mottled pattern of cattle hides shifting from year
    to year. She loved
      the droopy ruminant procession, allured,
        equally,

by purebred cacao-berry-brown bulls and heifers, or by calico
    mongrel bull-oxen,
      whether piebald black patches on white, or white on black
        (the mix of dark
    and light so blended, in many hides, who could say which
      was the dominant shade?). . . . One day, absently noting
        the interplay
      between cows and their reflected images,
        she woke

to epiphany! The mudblack ink scumming the surface, a light-
    impervious film,
      was a great leveller: all cattle—sepia, tan, or piebald—
        chomping the scrub
    of the riverbanks, saw ghost white twins of their heads
      and flanks in the river's mud mirror. Their tails wagged
        white flares, cud-
      chewing muzzles whitely ablaze. In Rio
        Bueno's

black mirror, all cows are white moons. Where the rivermuck feeds
    into the wide bay
      of Falmouth Harbor, the whole vast half-moon expanse turns
        mud, mud, mud!—far out
    to sea. . . . *Why Rio Bueno, I ask: apt name for mudslime*
      inferno of stinks? Oh, good for local traders, she scoffs!
        Named by Spaniards,
      in early days of Spanish rule. No shipments
        hijacked,

ever, by English pirates, sickened by pestilential odors. . . .
    The many rivers,
      nearing the seacoast, converge in the common mouth of Dunn's
        River Falls as spokes
    of a wheel merge in the hub, or spread fingers of a glove
      sewn in the palm cloth. . . .
                  The Martha Brae River, frothing

a personality
as vivid as its Anglican name, sizzles
and foams

and whitecaps around rocky breakwaters spaced, at wide intervals,
from its mountaintop
source to the falls: the last blowup in unstoppable melee
of whitewater flareups,
all fracas and blustery of temperament. In her baptismal
dousing, it is rumored, many a thief and pillager
was reborn
civic hero, or citizen reformer: Gods,
like humans,

after repeated dunkings, might change coats, or colors; underworld
demons and demigods
hatched into Apollos, Neptunes, or Jupiters. . . . Captain Morgan,
pirate-czar who robbed,
monthly, galleons of the Spaniards and beat upriver
retreats over Martha Brae's stormiest currents, flying
the rapids upstream,
always eluded the Spanish gunboat fleets
in pursuit

and fell in love with the River Goddess: Morgan, once a shipwrecked
castaway, master
of escape routes and princely of fugitives, mated—imagine it!—
to volatile Martha, she,
bordered with inlets and rimmed with secret harbors,
all havens for hideaways. . . . Legend has it, the Spanish
colonists—driven
hence—fled to Cuba, minus their treasures,
whereupon

skipper Morgan returned from three years' obscurity and exile,
transfigured by love's
lavings, love's wavelets and eddies, love's sandbars and algae
and starfish. Sporting
a forty-months grey beard, shoulders hidden in cascades
of curled locks, he emerged the people's statesman—
a landslide victory,
avalanche of votes. A reformed pirate elected
Governor! . . .

Today, his jilted paramour, vivacious to all who saddle her
  bucking wave-crests, wafts
 and floats the daily teams of rafts: cloth-lined rubber balloons,
  bamboo and osier-woven
log frames, old hollow wooden doors, solo daredevils
  on driftwood timbers, a few surfboard buffs, canoeists
   and paddleboard one-man
  dugouts; the rafters a cosmopolitan mix
   of natives

and foreigners, who turn out in greater numbers each year for raft
  river-speedways. The racers'
 stretch of whitewater rapids, like an Olympics skiers' trail
  beset with hazards, starts
in a mountain pool, the first runoff a wide mild falls
  giving a sharp launching boost to contestants. Many capsize,
   a few climbing ashore
  for treatment of wounds, or repairs of their craft.
   They drag

the rafts by ropes from the bank to the starters' plateau for second
  launchings (third or fourth,
 it may be), repeated capsizers disqualified after four failed
  tries. No races today!
But we can see flying specks and dotted wafers bobbing,
  at intervals, on strips of the river's ribboning zigzags
   visible in distant
  foothills. . . . The next wide band, glittery waterway,
   its course

a natural roller-coaster of switchbacks, loops, abrupt dips,
  vanishings in tunnels,
 detours around rock colossi, swerves into hidden recess,
  sheltered nook, inlet:
Rio Nuevo, site of the last cycle of battles,
  the fugitive half-crippled Spanish armada chased
   by British gunboats
  hiding for weeks at a stretch in obscure coves,
   camouflaged

by webworks of palmetto thatch shrewdly woven into sheets,
  tentlike shrouds

covering the beached vessels, while scattered remnants
    of Latins combined forces—
slowly, they mobilized for a last Kamikaze counter-
    offensive. The tribe of survivors, following the carnage,
        fled, via the nearby
        Green Grotto Caves (thereafter, dubbed *Runaway Caves*),
        to Cuba,

hurriedly patching together rafts from salvaged timbers hauled
        underground, chunks
    of mast and rigging (ropes, chains, charred sails) torn
        from the hull carcass
of wrecked galleons, bits and pieces sewn into patchwork
    sails for the Cuba-aimed rafts. Crawling from the cave burrows
        at dead of night
        like grave robbers or ghouls, skulking to the shaded
        river mouth

(midsummer overcast: the night moonless, starless), they drifted,
        downwind, across the bay
to open sea, slipping past the arrogant Anglo-captains,
        who, grown lackadaisical
and cocky in their conquest, supposed they'd exterminated
    every last Spanish patriot, thus allowing the small-scale
        downisland
        exodus. . . .
                Vámonos!—the last of Jamaica's
    Spanish-

speaking minority: the year 1658. . . . One hundred years' passage
    A fork-branch of Rio
Nuevo borders on a wealthy sugar plantation, the owner
    a deposed Voodoo
Queen—exiled from Haiti—taking on a succession
    of lovers, each chosen from jampacked stable of slaves.
        For two decades,
        fantastic rumors burgeon, tales of Obeah
        murders

by riverside, the ritual dismemberment of each slave lover
        when she tired of his charms,
    or sexual favors.

River burials of the corpse. Burials
of severed black limbs,
severed members. Slavewomen horrified by swollen flesh
geranium, surf-bobbed to shore following storm. The intact
puffy genital—
it is believed—seeks vengeance! Self-exhumed
from its grave

of water, it pursues the Haitian white witch—she strangled,
at last, in a slave
revolt. . . .
The liberated slaves found sanctuary, brief haven,
in the Runaway Caves.
Months later, after the lynch mobs and search parties quit
the hunt, the fugitives dug deep pit-traps for their pursuers
and slunk away upriver,
hugging the furrowed banks back to the river's
mountain-peak

source, and founding their own secluded hamlets, a permanent
freedmen's colony,
their heirs locked in the mind-set of eternal revolt against
the tyrant witchmistress.
Their cousins would claim squatters' rights on plantations
now owned and run by offspring of former slaves, the Rose Hall
Manor House left
standing: a haunted memorial to the defunct
slave era. . . .

6.

Now, tuned for last, she chants of the broadest whitewater artery,
if most distant from us—
the aristocrat! *Great River.*
The main channel a lunging basin catching runoffs
from two mountain ranges, its long quicksilver stretches—
ribboning from mountaintop
to seacoast—are interrupted by two sharp bends.
Torrents overflow the banks, flooding
pastures and plantations for miles on either side,
following storms. The worst recent storm, more river-
choking than the hurricanes—she recalls—
was ten months back. Downpour gush

massive and prolonged, flashfloods rampant, the risen maelstrom
      carried livestock (hoofs
      upturned, pointing skyward), whole
  shithouses intact, bobbing upright like phone booths
  afloat; just-cut stalks of harvested cane juggled and whipped
about the swirling surface,
      tens of thousands of stalks bounced on their tails
      like pickupstix, many hurled spearlike,
      impaling bulls, horses, sheep, or human passersby—
as tornado-driven straws pierce barnsides, fence
  posts. Banana sheds, thatchroofs torn off,
  were catapulted on shore rocks,

upchucking their contents, countless bananas radiating in tiers
      around the bound stalks
      interlaced in sheaves, now stripped
  of their green and yellow curved-finger-fruit thousands,
  hundreds ripping off per second, weightless in the fierce gales
as leaves or rose petals;
      banana sludge plastering the highways, windshields
      and sides of passing trucks, bridge cables
      and steel-frame crossed slats with shredded green peels
and yellow citrus splotches: tobacco leaves, mud, limes
  and pimento berries painting all exposed
  surface of the seashore

in a continuous banana-base fruit collage. She hymns a total-
      environment canvas
      as Jackson Pollock abstract! . . .
  Chickens and turkeys, by the coop-bushelfuls, spinning
  like tops, exposed wattle necks and pipecleaner jointed legs
poking above the surface,
      by turns; mixed eggyolk sprinkles and wind-whipped
      shellbit hails gorging the atmosphere
      of breathers like fine silica in the lungs of bauxite
miners. . . . She reports this comic storm of organic
  tidbits and particles, observed firsthand,
  she taking cover behind

a firm-rooted royal palm, the river-borne world of shrapnel
      debris roaring past. . . .
      She sees puffballs of chickenwire

rolling and somersaulting like mammoth tumbleweeds
over the locked melee of river-jam whipped contents; her eye
so bewitched by the carnival
> *display of sandwiched shapes and colors, dreamlike,*
> *fear and all thought of danger fall away,*
> *She feels absurdly free! She is an eggshell, yolkstained,*
dancing in spray tinged by the late low sun's rosé
> *pink glaze, and for moments, happily, she*
> *prays to be stripped of her rind,*

her heavy shell of skin and flesh. She would trade her frail bones
> *for the frailer curled*
> *half-shell of the egg, buffeted*
by wind and spray, so happy in the topsy-turvy
dance—spinning on itself without cease. . . . But the bottom
of the dream bursts upwards!
> The mainstays of the scene—walls of a theatre
> on opposite sides of the stage—
> collapse at once. No, she makes an effort over her eyes
to transcribe the optical mixup erupted into view. . . .
> The two bridge ends, slowly caving in, slant
> to the center. Cracks zigzag.

The foundations, at both sides, buckle, cement blocks shaken
> loose at the top, tossed
> this way and that like cardboard cubes.
> Caught in a whirlpool below, many roofs are tangled
in a coil—outhouses, chicken coops, banana sheds, sugar-
cane and tobacco huts—
> each roof typified by a unique design, but outlines
> blurred in the hodgepodge jumble
> of eaves, split rafters, ridgepoles, loosed nails, sheet tin
and zinc squares. . . . All are mud-glued in a vast hoop-shape!
> Cartwheeling like the blade of a giant chainsaw
> into the bridge midsection,

it hurtles against frame and suspended roadway. The third charge—
> adding chunks of concrete
> and timbers to the roof cartwheel's
combined mass—heaves the bridgepiles inward at both
> extremities, and, in less than a flicked eyeblink, bursts
the bridgeframe at the center,

the two severed halves of highway jackknifed upwards
(now she'd recalled seeing segments
of Miami causeway, upraised in slow motion, those lips
of black asphalt sensuously parted to give berth
to tall masts of the approaching sailboat
in a Florida film travelog),

leaving a trucksized gap in the middle, the long bauxite-heaped
truck, its hill of ore
forming a smallish cone-shaped peak,
still intact, visible a few yards above the trailer top.
The twelve-wheel steel chassis horizontal yet, as if parachuted
from above, slowgliding, drops
through the widening slot. It caps the mound of flotsam
and is swept, whirling, out to sea.
The driver, his expression dazed but head and shoulders unbudged
behind the steering wheel, switches on windshield wipers,
blinking *hazard* lights, turn signal, and rotates
lit spotlight beam—his eyes aglow,

expectant. . . . In his trance, the dashboard combination of gadgetry
should quickly correct
the disordered highway cosmos. . . .
A thin trail of exhaust smoke, spiralling higher
and higher from his diesel smokestack, is starkly visible, still,
long after the truck—tumbled
from the heap—has plunged into the sea. . . . Fear shatters
the swollen bubble of her fantasia
of images. She runs from riverbank to high ground, for safety
from ravaging floodwaters, never once glancing back
over her shoulder to survey aftershocks
of the bridge dismantlement. . . .

7.

At daybreak, thick bags of provisions
and paratroopers
could be seen
dropping from a fleet
of giant metallic wasps
(*helicopters*, she heard them named
later that morning), hundreds
of homeless wayfarers arriving—

from all parishes
of countryside—to receive
doled handouts
from the U. S. Marines. The peasants
and farmers, I knew from her story's tone,

were more bountiful in their thankyous
than the beefy troops
who meted out
my country's "care packets"
and Red Cross supplies. *Manna.*
Her eyes now grant *me* thanks, unearned,
on behalf of my fellow
countrymen in spiffy uniforms,
that militia
of aiders. . . . Later that morning,
the choppers
dangling steel hooks from chains, bunched
in squads of three and four, dragged the dozen,

or so, jigsaw chunks of metal framework
and pavement amalgam
topped with slabs
of marl-based tarmac (the latter
resembling the ruins
of mammoth blackboards) from Great River's
debris-clogged basin. One by one,
the airborne demolitions crew grappled
and carted away
one-hundred-ton wedges and jagged
pie slices
of dismembered bridge, loading the webbed
girders and steel-beam sections in teetery heaps

stacked on the beach adjacent to fallen
bridge pylons. The high-piled
units, towering
over nearby royal palms—
asway in moderate winds—seemed
a child's prank of balancing Tinker Toys
or erector sets. . . . Some pilots,
endeared to local pals, returned, months

later, to construct
the new bridge, working side by side
with native crews,
humming reggae tunes, and bandying tales
of the storm that unleashed Great River's Demon. . . .

ODE TO THE RUNAWAY CAVES

(Ocho Rios, Jamaica)

1.

Approaching the caves, we shuffle
    down a long path—
    bark
and leafneedle bestrewn: our course winds
    between aisles of trees,
    criss-
crossings of thick vines overhead drooped,
    at times, to our knees,
    ankles. . . .
We must take high steps, or crawl below!
    The taller pimento trees,
    skins
unscrolling like eucalyptus rinds,
    give way to palms,
    old trunks.
The thick boles—sickly, rotted—languish
    in the embrace of creaturely
    sidewinders:
trees sprung from sky like air plants, trees
    hung from the shoulders
    and necks
of quickly aging mates, draining the saps,
    sucking out the mineral
    enzymes. . . .
Anaconda and vampire!
                It strangles a donor
    tree even as it sips
    bole blood—
then stretches its many aerial plunger
    stems to earthward,
    puts down
stays for anchorage, and deserts the host—
    left to crumple, collapsing
    slowly
into dry-rot hollows. . . .
                That distant cousin
    to the copious banyan—the fig,
    the fig!

2.

Corkscrewing down the long tubular stairwell, we descend
      sixty-odd steps
      of the spiral ladder
(the steel frame inserted in the deep narrow shaft
in the rock, a natural chute affording passage to all
three cave levels), eyes
      of each riveted to the next footfall: the head
      of the Swiss child below, her locks
      bobbing just under my halt instep; two German
dowagers above—hefty *Fräuleins*—bickering
      over the slow pace, floppy sandals
      grazing my brow, now and again;

our guide posted one floor below the thin floor we file through—
      gophers dropping
      down a burrow—grips
each pilgrim under the elbow (the last step
is overlong), or he lifts the children down with hands
cupped under hips
      and motions to clasp, likewise, the twenty-year-old
      blond Canuck from Quebec,
      her eyes spurning his advance as she swerves—wordless
in her dodge—past his outstretched forearms: smitten,
      he turns in a crouch admiring her thighs,
      no one to break my shortfall,

I following the checked pass, my footing shaky. . . . *Third level.*
      The lowest cave
      basement. Or may this floor,
    ceiling to still another tunnel, collapse
    underfoot? We pause a few moments, letting our eyes
adjust to dimmed light,
      the few widely scattered electric bulbs spaced out
      over the high cave roof. Zigzagging,
      feeble as birthday-cake candles, the bluish eggs cast
small patches of dull-grey glow on the ceilings:
      the light recoils, trapped in overhead
      pulsing ovals—it falls back

on its source. . . . But now, the broad dimensions of our earth-
      cavity limn

themselves on the black ink
impenetrable sea of rock far to the left
and right, and to a great misty distance ahead. We take
our first sheepish steps.
    The floor vanishes. It sinks under our footfalls.
    We seem to proceed, unmoving,
    against the black immobile backdrop. A shimmer-
halo capsules our troop. We drift, weightless,
    as if enclosed in a foamy nimbus
    of half-light, ellipsoidal

balloon that lifts us and carries us forward, so far below
    earth's crust we dream
    our limbs free of gravity,
    as if we ride on a satellite orbiting
    outside the atmosphere. Distant arched cave-walls loom,
hazily, into view
    (I think of low-ceilinged excavated walls of mines)—
    abruptly, we bear left, our guide
    leading us single file toward a pool of brighter light.
Magnetized, we are drawn into the widening lit
    circle—our invisible knees, legs,
    and feet refleshed. We duck!—

shrinking to elude a heavy flapping of wings overhead, one
    winged shadow-pouch
    hurtling so close to my face
    I feel its wind-puffs fanning my ears and wave
    my arms, shooing away the attacker. Then, we hear
wing-bursts zoom upwards,
    the blind flyers shifting their course to avoid us.
    Rockets! Taking right-angled turns,
    they dive straight into a gap in the cave-roof, the flood
of direct sunlight striking their outspread wing-tops
    with a near-physical impact. The bats'
    wings—braking their ascent

to an utter halt—shudder, as if so much raw brightness
    were a solid wall,
    the light's body thudding
    heavily upon their backs—an invisible mass
    weighing, weighing. We make out three or four bats, clumped
closely together,

battling fiercely against the light-barrier, sun's
gleaming steel repulsing wave
after wave of their terrible failed climb, failed exodus;
we sidling near, the better to witness the air show,
shocked at the size of the crumpled wings
beating in place. Giant birds

of the underworld! Bats large as crows, Hades' blind offspring
hang suspended,
their black iridescent wings,
sun-speckled, lost in a limbo of stuckness,
heaving, trapped between two unseen archenemies—
sun and man, twin satans
of bat-purgatorio. Then, by a common will,
four angry black blots—shrunken,
wings folded into nothing, buried in deep pockets,
buried in emptiness—plunge in perfect formation,
divebombing our naked upturned
faces, four guided missiles

diving as one. We flinch, twelve targets huddled as one, arms
upswung to shield
our eyes; and we crouch, back-
stepping from the charmed circle of light, sungush
pouring through the magic aperture—a circuit of slots
in three cave-roofs
admitting a barrel-wide column of unimpeded light.
Bravely, we shuffle the few steps
back into the lit-floor oasis. Hand-visors cupped
over our brows (in mock-salute to Sol), we search
for hovering black lumps, or flung bulbs
swooping in vertical bat-trails

amid traceries of vines dangling from out-of-sight trunks
or shrubs, anchored
to a near-forgotten sky
of earth-crust. Now we hear the bats zinging
and humming, anew, in swift horizontal air-laps, wings
grazing our necks and ears. . . .
Our eyes stay trained to the vertical wonders,
the guide tracing with the wand
of his index finger the outlines—looping up and down—
of record-length stalactites and stalagmites,

two of the latter extending upwards
from the cave-floor, pinnacle

vertex towering almost twice the height of the tallest man
in our party. One
inverted steeple—its spire
dropping to our waists—is fastened to a sunken roof
recessed in a thirty-foot-high arch topping the limits
of our sight. The stone
icicles (all uppers *and* downers), fashioned
from calcium drippings, lengthen
at a speedy one-thousand-years-per-inch. But what
are these tough cables, anchored below and above,
I ask, yanking quarter-inch-thick pipes,
lifting my weight on one by one—

vines, stems, tubers? Figtree roots, split into many offshoots,
each hunting water,
threading hundreds of feet
through slits and burrows, attaching to damp surface—
they are glued stuck with a firmness of welded steel joints!
The hardy fig—born
an airplant, a parasite—locks its long talons
of roots into a mature tree-mate,
dehydrates the host slow-sipping away its life, drops
tendrils to earth and begins its second birth,
late trunks replacing the host-tree's
rotted corpus. And now we see

two long dangling fig-roots just overhead, looping and twisting.
Blind snakes! Forked ends
(tongueless, but on the scent)
grope for fecund damp of wells, cave-swamps, cave-lakes,
hidden breeding grounds, deep-dug to befit the ancient fruit.
Survivor. Mate-slayer.
Master of the drink and drought, tough in stock, root
and seed, your fruit is wholesome to eat—
plump or dried, fresh-picked or aged, preserved in cellars,
forerunner to our modern date or prune. *Ancestor!*
Lawrence marvelled at your manybranched
slitherings over the bare rocks

of Taormina, worshipped that sufficiency in endless brood—
able to beget
ever more shoots of shoots,

each root progenitor to families of others, others!
But little guessed he this illicit netherworld root-farm
of the overland creeper,
    doubling its purlieu to above and below, the one tree
    versatile as a swarm of kingsnakes.
And now two eyeless snake-heads venture forth, wayfaring
from a trunk earth-socketed sixty feet above,
    the tree's exposed top a mere fraction
    of its serpentining root-life.

3.

Drawn to a network
    of markings, dimly visible
    on one wall beside the skylight,
we walk single file—stooping
for a closer look at the broken silhouettes.
        Bestial figures in murals?
At first, we avail ourselves of overhead light
filtering down
            through multiple layers
of ceilings and casting
faint glimmers on two or three nearest panels. Our guide,

at last, unboxes
    a trove of welcome supplies.
    Inching backwards, we follow survived
patches of line-drawings
down a narrow winding corridor, aided by candles,
        mine guttering in the small dish
cupped in my unsteady hand. The lower drawings, etched
in rock levels
            parallel to our knees,
waists, chins—no higher!—
are still finely delineated, some splotches of color lost

or flaking off,
    iridescent flecks winking
    on bordered profiles: dull orange faces,
antique brownish hides,
the few sparkles hinting outer limits of figures—
        man or beast—outlines faded
or blurred. A dull patina of color residues marks out
special features yet—

eyes, nostrils, hair; blood flow
into pools, blood drippings,
blood coagulated beneath the torso of the just-slain ox

or wildcat. The men,
 portrayed, are squat and pudgy,
  their dwarfish stature divulged by waist-low
drafts of their cave-murals
(as measured against our own upright frames, huddled
  so close to walls we can sniff
crumpled pigments)—scene of the hunt, hand-to-hand combat,
feast-days: tableaux
  of Arawak tribal-art. . . .
We come to a blank
interval, and pause, groping for stable foothold. The space

between walls shrinks,
 but our guide bids us proceed.
 Soon, a pattern of starker images unfolds
at the level of our heads
and higher, some figures extending so far upwards
  only three or four tallest men
in our group can view, clearly, the topmost scenes: line-
drawings; the few strokes
  of this taller Race condense
detail, the contours
and shapes of creatures hinted by dotted outlines. Muscle arc

here. Lower jaw-line
 there. Thickness of line defines
 movement, collisions between figures, angle
of stance—a far cry
from the fine lacework of design and color palette
  of the pygmy Race who inked
and pigment- spattered the low murals we met before. (No one
knows, for certain,
  how old are the top-level
minimalist chalk
drawings: the style—lean and pared of excess—is signature,

I surmise, of Carib
 tribes who lived tens of thousands
 of years prior to recorded alphabets. Pre-

Indian cave-dwellers). . . .
Wait! What crawls here? What writhes across the walls,
in waves? The whole cave-wing buckles.
The drawings leap! They shudder, twisting in the candle-
flickered tall flumes
of light fanning out wider,
and dimmed, in the cave
upper reaches. The columns of light flare in and out (X-rays

of lungs inflated, lungs
deflated), while the drawings sway
from side to side. . . . On the return trek,
I note a few incurved panels
matching up artworks of both eras, the one stacked
over the other, a few inches
between the upper and lower murals—the newer scenes
incised with care
under their ghostly consorts,
so narrow the space
closing a breach of millennia between Races of cave mammals

(breeds of bipeds,
both more or less upright). . . .
The midget descendants—so many family
lifelines removed from Sires,
now rivals—fitted their neat blocked-out designs,
minutely, below the counterparts
of Great Uncles. . . . *Boasts or tributes? Did they fancy over-*
wrought detail-work
and ornament superior
to matchless taut strokes
of their forerunners? Or did they guess their art outclassed?

4.

The bats, in greater numbers than ever,
start zinging
and flapping about our ears. . . .
We enter a wide central space, juncture
where many arms
of the cave honeycomb merge:
dodging those black vampiric swoopers,
I slip

on a curled wet leaf
(no banana peels here!), which quakes
    and slithers
        under my shoe-sole's graze.
I lower my candlewick. The footlong lizard,
    softskinned,
        is joined by two moist fellow
streakers, chasing each other up one wall,
    then zigzagging
        back to the floor (sides
puffing in and out, throats ballooning,
    at intervals):
        sure-toed and speedy
on wall climbs or floorscootings, segmented
    toe-digits
        visibly curling, uncurling,
little sockets perfectly fluid. Errless. . . .
    Not lizards!
        Too puffed-up and fleshy.
Giant eyeless salamanders.
                Extra bodysize
    recompense
        for loss of sight? But blindness
is no curse in these unlighted vaults,
    not dungeons
        to those who—deprived
from birth of sky   earth   weather—
    combine
        the fluidities of runners,
swimmers, and flying beings into the one
    all-purpose
        slithery quickstep, a walk
that is half slide, half float. . . .
                The fleet
    of a dozen
        outsize salamanders
is followed by jumping blind roaches, thick
    as frogs,
        not stumbling on many overlarge
legs. . . .
        Now we traverse the longest tunnel,
    light-
        flickers on a pool of water

edging into view at the far end. Our guides
      recite
          lessons in speleology—
more intoned, or sung, than spoken—
      each pilot
          holding forth to his troop:
two clumped galleries, we advance, now,
      in a pair
          of loosely intact divisions.
Our three-quarter-mile circuit, we're
      reminded,
          is a mere token sampling
of seven miles of caves, gouged and carved
      by sea
          currents, the whole honeycomb
submerged below two hundred feet of water.
      In trance,
          we think our way back
to knives of currents and swells cutting
      the grooves
          and boring the trenches
in solid rock that became a labyrinth.
      Chainsaws!
          Hacksaws of all-eating
acidic brines and rock-piercing salts,
      corrosive
          to hardest quartz or flint.
A feat of rock-sculpture! . . .
                        Following
      the cave-craft
          exercise, the sea withdrew
(architect departed, but near his creation),
      survived
          by a second maze of six
underground pools, all interlaced, topped
      by "Mr. Lake,"
          dark pond we skirted past
at ground level, prior to our spiralled
      descent—
          the deepest lake in Jamaica,
its many subterranean outflows and runoffs
      funnelled
          into the six buried lakes.

5.

We step into a cavern,
the high-roofed iglooshape crowned
by a dome—ceiling to a vast, oval, sunken lake
adjacent to the narrow shelf
we stand upon, hovering over the lake-
edge to stare
at our eerie rippling faces
reflected in the glowing sheen
of the lake's black mirror.
Our stone footledge a pocked and cratered wharf,
jetty of the interior?—
we dodge small tidepools scattered
here and there, which—chants our guide—refill
each dawn when the risen sea-
tides lift the sunken lake, as well,
to its morning
high water mark.
We advance,
slowly, in bands of threes,
to moorings of rowboats,
two small vessels secured by ropes, the guides
each taking installments
of three passengers for "a spin," a few
circlings of the pool. . . .
Even as the first boat inches
from the improvised dock, I'm lulled
in a trance of recall: *when, in whose dream,*
have I unmoored—
oars in the gunwales, rowing out
from this ghost-pier to the center
of a roofed body
of water calm as sheet glass? I'm hunting in memory,
still, when the guide
tongues nostalgias of his fast friendship
with the noble Scotsman, Sean Connery, formed during unnumbered
takes for the few cave-lake scenes
in the premiere Bond flick, *Dr. No,* a Soul-
Brother love
redoubled in later rehearsals
for *Live and Let Die.* Now erect,
he jabs with one oar

submerged vertically, as a Venetian gondolier poles
a gondola from shore. . . .

*   *   *

The surface looks so opaquely black
  I feel as if our bow is a knife-edge, the little boat
    an ice-cutter slicing its slow path
      through ink-black ice, or through a slate
    of petrified dinosaurs
  and pterodactyls. . . .
        The oarsman,
      now stirring only faintest ripples
  in a flawless surface,
    drops one oar, taking up with his free hand a portable
spotlight (battery-
generator tucked in the handle),
    and points the projected beam directly below. He stabs
      to such depths so close to shore
        the very lake-margins seem bottomless,
      the light streaking
    past the limits of sight. But the lit
        column of water, so pure and stirless,
      takes on deep color,
    and we are cutting through green-black shale, milky-black
chalcedony; the light
a laser-beam drilling through stone
or steel, with equal ease.
          Now he swings the lamp
      to and fro like a lantern—two slow
        swimmers pop into view at once, crisscrossing,
    the curvy snake-shape
    moving at right angles to the fish below,
        their even course not a trace deflected
    by the high-powered beam.
    "Are they perfectly tame, or drifting asleep, if mobile?"—
inquires the German duchess
from Duttersdorf (sixtyish and mated
    to her coquette travelling companion, just out of her teens—
      nubile); the man at the oars, chary,
        who flirts with all women and a few
    young boys, demurs,
    addressing these two in deadpan voice,

slow drawl pitched for a pair
of neuters, or eunuchs:
"No. Both blind," comes the reply. "Blind perch. Blind eel."
So saying, he follows
the snakelike glider to lower depths
tracing the sluggish trajectory of its dive—his lightbeam's
lazy-slow descent, a ritardando,
paced by the droopy tempo of his spiel. . . .
Both species—scaly fish
and snakefish alike—evolved over a stretch
of lightness cave-aeons. Neither met
by natural enemies,
nor Killer-humans. Both protected, today, by strict Island
Edict. Thus! Drift,
peaceably blind, from birth to death.
(Feeding, no doubt, think I, on saintly blind plankton.). . . .

* * *

A large crayfish, distant relation
to the clawless Florida lobster, grabs
the submerged oar-tip
and starts to crawl backwards. It slips
on the slick wood, straddles the edge
with many legs pressed
tight, now resumes its creep *down* the upwards-pointed oar
approaching the wrist
gripping its shaft—the guide showing off
the blind crustacean's viselike grip and adroitness
in the climb, descent or ascent
all one to those hairlike antennae checking,
blindly checking. . . .
Four bats, chasing each other
across the lake-face, charge
the concave walls,
the roof blinking in and out of the swung lamp-beam
charting their wavery arcs.
Without slowdowns, they brake to a standstill
just inches this side of walls. Batswoops start and stop
at full speed, arrow streaks
the only moves those flung black blots
think in their wing-
bones. Far more exact than sight,

bats' radar! No bats collide
　　　with panes of glass
　　　　as sighted birds strike windows—flawless their skill
　　in bouncing echoes. . . .

*   *   *

We are skimming faster and faster,
　　　　our boatman racing breakneck into the cavern's rear wall
　　　　　　lacking batskill at sudden halts—
　　　　　　　　at the last instant, he plays a trick
　　　　　　with the twisted oars:
　　　　　we come about, a hairpin turn
　　　　　　　　　as deft as a sailboat's tack in gale
　　　　　winds; and we glide,
　　　　　　hugging the cave-wall so close I can sniff the stone's damp
　　coarse skin, my knuckles
brushing the moss and lichen sprouted
　　　　therefrom. Our rower follows exact wavy contours of wall, fractions
　　　　　　of an inch between gunwale and rock
　　　　　　　　though he looks to the side, or faces one
　　　　　　passenger, another,
　　　　　engaged in repartee. . . .
　　　　　　　　　　　How does he keep
　　　　　　　a parallel course, I wonder, never bumping
　　　　the undulant wall
　　　or swerving away? Does he, too, read the echoes, tutored
by his bat-escorts
of two decades: men exchange messages
　with whales, dolphins—but not bats! . . .
　　　　　　　　　　　He drops both oars and rises
　　　　　to his feet, the boat not tipping—
　　　　　　　come to rest in hidden nook. Odd music begins.
　　　　　He taps with his palms
　　　and finger pads. Cushions of his thumbs
　　　　　　　look spongy-sensitive (possum or raccoon
　　　　paws I have seen,
　　　exploring forage or nest-provisions with a touch
so soft and feather-
light): he thumps, gently, on a wide,
　　　hollow stalactite, top half embedded in the wall, bottom half
　　　　　　suspended like an icicle, the shell
　　　　　　　　wavy, S-curved as if it housed a row of tall

cylinders or tubes
all connected.
                    A series of organ pipes!
          Though his handpats roll lazyslow,
      trembles of a bongo-
          drummer, resonant scales that issue from the stone skins
      mimic organ notes;
his throat's guttural hums and groans,
          in timbre with his palm-thumpings, knuckle-raps, simulate
              organ valves, organ pedals pumping;
                    while the cave-dome is the great organ loft
              in Chartres Cathedral.
          Eyes shut, I hear Gaston Litaize
                    command the instrument, two or three
              dozen pipe-throats
          all singing at once. Cathedral roof and arched cupolas
      return matched counter-
song in Saint-Saens' orotund Third:
          echoes upon echoes, so paced by an organist, are the instrument's
              cloak, its garment and accompanist.
                    Cathedral and organ, cave-dome and stalactite,
              wedded in duets—
          voice of the first partner so woven
                    with the second, who can tell where
              the blent song begins,
          where it ends? . . .
                              We are rowing again, glued to wall borders,
      looping into hollows
and tracing the stone perimeter
          as if our bowsprit were a lobster's eye-stalk, tip of a superior
              sight organ. But the rower looks away.
                    He lets the bow crawl to its own tune: "Old
              Cathedral Rock,"
          he intones, again and again, pleased
                    with his name for the organ-stalactite
          he concertizes upon.
          He is naming a Spirit, his instrument shared with us. Voice
      of the place. A personage.
We stop by a chain of long rock-icicles,
          arranged in a pattern, roughly, of graduated larger widths.
              "Cave Man Piano," he cheerily dubs
                    this unorthodox keyboard, and rolls the knuckles
              of both hands

from side to side, the notes emitted
                mixing pops and tinkles and runs—
an upright xylophone!
    His tongue clicks accompaniment, completing a jazz ensemble.
One by one, we advance
to each new species of music sampling
        stalactites of all shapes and dimensions, each christened
            with its own apt name: "Limbo Drum."
                "Rasta Roll Chimney." "Calypso Jim Chatterbox."
        We applaud each jewel
        in the repertoire.
                            All jumping to our feet
                at once, we clap hands for an encore—
        the boat nearly capsized,
    we drop in our seats with a great plop! Four vacationers' rumps
afford enough ballast
to restore our all-but-swamped vessel's
        balance. His recital ended, the maestro—too caught up in virtuoso
            songfest to notice we'd shipped gallons
                and gallons of water—now sets to pitching
            scooped bucketfuls
        over the side, we frozen to our seats,
                the boat still asway.
                            The two *Fräuleins*

        seated in the stern-bench,
    cup their hands together and ladle small palmfuls of spillage,
flinging the contents
back over their shoulders; too absorbed,
    perhaps, in their frenzied waist-bends and heaves to notice
            that I remain still, if wide-eyed,
                jailed in a trance more active than hull-
            drainage furor . . . .

                        *   *   *

                    The searchlight,
        dropped to bowseat during the music solos,
                now switched to the dial's brightest setting
            in the scuffle, rolls
        to and fro on the bench, in time with the seesawing of the boat.
    As we drift, slowly,
back to port the power-beam flashes
        from wall to wall, roof to pool, pool-face to lake-depths:

this ongoing kaleidoscope of lights
and shadows meshes, at last, with the dim—
but flickery—overhead
one-hundred-watt bulbs strung out on wires
hung like so many Christmas-tree ornaments
from the lower roof
topping the makeshift dock. The exquisite play of the lights,
above and below, is magic
counterpart to the quelled festival
of sounds, extinguished moments before, as if the echoes
and multiple re-echoings of the orchestra
of stalactite percussion family—drums, cymbals,
timpani, castanets,
xylophone—sunk into the silence,
returns in another form: the lightshow
before my eyes! . . . The ripples
and small waves, stirred by our fracas, still radiate outwards
from the lake's back end.
Our boat—stationed at the rear quadrant
when we swamped the hull-floor—coasted, by a direct radius,
across the long oval sweep of water
shoreward; but the cycle of waves and small swells,
touched off by our rocking
and seesaw maneuvers, pursues our craft
to its moorings and persists long after.
Now wave-ripples catch
periodic glares of the spotlight, whereupon the lake-face
is floodlit, in surges,
like a stage show. . . .
I'm held, transfixed,
by tossings back and forth of reflections, the cave-roof aglow
with mirrorings cast by the wave-pulse,
confusing roof and floor.
Stalactites and roof-craters
change places with waves
and splashed light-sparkles. Oval expanse
of wet flickers over our heads, a lake
ceiling suspended,
safely, thirty or forty feet above; while an arched stone roof,
reversed in concavity,
is fallen below our legs. Our profiles
are cast above and below: heads and furrowed shoulders appear,

one moment, in a shuffled tile-mosaic
on the roof; our belt-buckles, knees, and sandals
glow, the next moment,
in a patchwork quilt collage on the floor
of wet spray, below. . . .

6.

Back in line, my head still spinning with the lights bounced
to and fro between cave-
      roof and lake-face, we stall
for a long moment,
waiting for the two guides to choose between five tunnels
      for our departure and ascent
back to the sky of ground zero. The low chamber
in our rear, our gate
      of entry to the mushroom-shaped great dome,
      is joined by four other cave wings
which radiate

like glove fingers from the oval cavern. The bloated slow guide
chooses first. He leads
      his single file troopers
into the low-roofed,
thickest channel, the glove's wide thumb. In the few moments'
      delay before *we* proceed
to the narrower—if highest—tunnel (the hand's
index finger),
      the spotlight beam directed from the boat's
      bowscat, still oscillating, casts
a row of shadows

over the heads of those passing through the exit. Silhouettes
etched on the far wall
      loom tall as giants, lanky,
their elongated heads
and aquiline noses dimmer than the overbroad shoulders;
      while a second set of shadows
projected on the near wall by the string
of overhead bulbs,
      moving at the same tempo as the Race
      of Goliaths, exhibits flat
melon-shaped skulls,

thickset squat carriage, their legs oddly arched. They hobble
on the bandy legs,
        a Race of dwarfs. Their dark
shadow-bodies
look husky compared to the diaphanous-grey torsos,
        translucent, of their long-boned
twin brethren, the two Races of cave-dweller
muralists returned
        from widely divergent epochs. Their arms
        now upraised, members of each stock
wave a salute

to their kin! Two clans of cave-folk, apparitional, at peace
in the underworld, greet
        each other across mute Gulfs,
their grand meeting
ignored by the fleshly Race, trapped in their Chamber-
        of-Commerce Tour. Obtuse to forefathers
trading amenities filtered through our moderners'
witless shadows,
        our band of hikers resumes its lax pace.
        Before I can instruct my numb tongue
in words to share

my vision, I blanch to my hair-roots, sensing *my* hand, too,
raised of itself—unwilled—
        in salute to my cave Ancients,
fellow bipeds
snatched from oblivion. Perhaps their many lifted palms
        hold pigments, chalks poised to draft
more wall sagas. . . . *Both flocks of shadow-folk halt,*
in lockstep. Hands
        lowered, they begin a retreat, back-
        stepping slowly. Then aboutface!
They all pivot

on their heels, and running in reverse, a few souls trip
on both walls at once—
        but it's the hikers between walls,
now in panic, who
return—crowding in their haste—to the long cavern,
        a woman near the front of their ranks

breaking out in howls, calmed to soft yelps by a help-
mate's pooh-poohings.
    The chain reaction of fright triggered a mass
    exodus, but all fear quickly melts
to laughter—while I

mourn for the sudden fadeout of both shadow Races, shrunk
back into the walls
       they graced in life with bison,
jackal, aurochs,
and mountain lion, the same walls they flitted across
    for breathless moments of hailed
hand-greetings to fellows across Time. Those images
drown in the cave-rock,
    sunk as swiftly as the blind eels and perch
    which, crisscrossing our spotlight beam,
dove to lake depths.

7.

      Our Ace
  spelunker, still in titters over the Quebec
      blond's terror of the buzzard
fallen into the deep cave stairwell (her rescuer,
    himself), cheers me with whispered details of the fracas.
      The prey-fowl,
  its vast wingspread clogged and flapping,
      had ripped out wingtip plumes
in a struggle to free itself from narrow confines
    of the man-dug burrow (our intended exit chute); its beak
    blood-flecked,
a trickle of blood dripping from its bruised
    bulb-head. . . .
              A lame vulture,
overlarge, sickly, and old! But the City girl,
    seeing face droplets still moist (*gorging on which blood
    type—mammal
quadruped or biped?*), supposed the bird
      to be a monster vampire-bat,
a horribly enlarged mutant of the giant breed
    we'd met at the start of our hike. . . .
              Now both rows

of pilgrims
follow their mentors, our smaller troop led
through a narrow high passageway
to our chosen exit-hatch; and again, the shadows
aflicker, I'm braced as ever to witness comings and goings
of past tenants.
Our guide, taunted or dared by a wager,
quickens our pace: a fast trot
escalates to a slow run, amid threats by senior
spelunkers who feel trapped between fear of tripping
in hidden ruts
and dread of being left behind for lost. . . .
At a few gaps in our tunnel's
right wall, we're surprised to behold our companion
line-up scuttling in a course parallel to ours; and later,
I catch glimpses
through small portholes in the other wall:
an obscure band of Islanders
four to five deep, rudely bumping each other
in their haste, are running in the opposite direction,
their wider tunnel,
too, juxtaposed with ours. . . .
Are they fugitives?
Who are they fleeing? I, alone,
seem to notice the native runaways—hanging back
for a peek at those in pursuit.
In the eyes of this gang,
true agony!
Not for a moment, sport, or fake *angst* trumped up
to fool the lone peephole
voyeur. . . .
Do I recognize their costumes from drawings
or color plate etchings in Island history texts—the halfcaste
striped greys,
compulsory uniform of slaves?
My lord! The style
went out with eighteenth-century
sugar plantations, following the ritual murders
of three sugar barons, top-echelon slave traders. The instant
I decipher
the runners' style of dress, they vanish
before my eyes. . . .

Clippity-clop

of wooden clogs grows louder. Nearer. I clap hands
over my ears. The vacuum left by the disembodied black racers
doubles my pulse.
Ah! Their shadows, bare-chested now, are flying
over the walls, wave after wave
of runaways, their terror now mine. The shadows'
silhouettes so keenly detailed, I'll always remember three
or four faces—
those faces in dreams we've known all our lives
(or longer), but who? We cannot say.
That washboard corrugation of a tall man's ribs!
Stark receding forehead of the hook-nosed man. Those shadow-
figures hurtle
across the walls, again and again. Identical.
The same profiles, always running
in the one direction, never beating a retreat
or stopping for breath, the shadow outlines blurred, at last. . . .
Bat runaways
veer, in formation, their squadrons zigzagging
in and out of the human fugitives'
shadows. . . .
The refugees are running on a treadmill,
I fear, or conveyor belt always moving in reverse. It turns
at variable speed,
matching the pace of the runners, offsetting
their escape, while they run in place.
But now, as I watch, the principals are changing,
each new wave of shadows relaying a new host of actors:
new vigilantes
in the chase, new escapees on the run—for moments,
in each wave, the figures chiselled
in luminous outline, their exact features knife-edged
black on the cloud-grey backdrop.
Incisive profiles!

Columbus
and his brothers, invincible, laughing in escape
with their plunder, crown jewels
and doubloons stolen from the British ships, smuggled
through the vertigo maze of runaway caves.
Now straggler Spaniards,

last survivors

of the fatal gunboat battles with the Britons,
                     steal back (through the network
of caves) to the one saved ship, hidden
              and camouflaged in an obscure cape of the Rio Nuevo, sanctuary
              just inland
from the cave exits. Later, they will sail
              to Cuba—never to return (today,
no Spanish in Jamaica). . . .
                  Once more, the slave runaways
         appear, fugitives from British sugar magnates. Many, captured,
         will perish.
Others, biding their cave time, will migrate
               uphill into colorful mountain
coast ranges, so to found their own settlement
            of the sunken interior . . .
                  Maroon Country.

ABOUT THE AUTHOR

Laurence Lieberman has been widely anthologized; his poems and critical essays have appeared in most of the country's leading magazines—*The New Yorker*, *The American Poetry Review*, *The Hudson Review*, and *Sewanee Review* among them. The poetry editor for the University of Illinois Press and professor of English at the University of Illinois, he is the author of three previous books of poetry, *The Unblinding* (1968), *The Osprey Suicides* (1973), and *God's Measurements* (1980), as well as a collection of essays on contemporary poets, *Unassigned Frequencies: American Poetry in Review* (1978). He was awarded an Illinois Arts Council Fellowship for 1982.